CW00554407

British Battles 4

British Battles 493–937

Mount Badon to Brunanburh

by Andrew Breeze

ANTHEM PRESS

Anthem Press
An imprint of Wimbledon Publishing Company
www.anthempress.com

This edition first published in UK and USA 2021
by ANTHEM PRESS
75–76 Blackfriars Road, London SE1 8HA, UK
or PO Box 9779, London SW19 7ZG, UK
and
244 Madison Ave #116, New York, NY 10016, USA

First published in the UK and USA by Anthem Press in 2020

Copyright © Andrew Charles Breeze 2021

The author asserts the moral right to be identified as the author of this work.

All rights reserved. Without limiting the rights under copyright reserved above,
no part of this publication may be reproduced, stored or introduced into
a retrieval system, or transmitted, in any form or by any means
(electronic, mechanical, photocopying, recording or otherwise),
without the prior written permission of both the copyright
owner and the above publisher of this book.

British Library Cataloguing-in-Publication Data
A catalogue record for this book is available from the British Library.

Library of Congress Control Number: 2021937591

ISBN-13: 978-1-83998-070-1 (Pbk)
ISBN-10: 1-83998-070-2 (Pbk)

This title is also available as an e-book.

To my mother and to the memory of my father

CONTENTS

INTRODUCTION

This book is about war, and specifically about early battlefields in Britain. Some of its material has appeared in historical journals (as shown in the bibliography); other chapters are previously unpublished. All of them break new ground. They relate, for example, the British victory over West Saxons at Mount 'Badon' in 493 to Braydon in north Wiltshire; the massacre of an allied Scottish-Irish force at 'Degsastan' in 603 to Wester Dawyck, southern Scotland; the Northumbrian defeat at *Maserfelth* in 642 to Forden, near Welshpool; and the English triumph at *Brunanburh* in 937 to Lanchester, County Durham. The traditional locations proposed for these battles (Badbury, Dawston Rigg, Oswestry, Bromborough) can hence be rejected.

If arguments for such places are compelling, there are three main benefits. First, much Anglo-Saxon history can be rewritten. We shall understand better the aims of commanders on both sides and their success (or lack of it). Second is an advance for archaeologists. They need not waste time excavating a site in mid-Wiltshire or the Wirral in a quest for swords and spears, because they would be looking in the wrong place. Third is the demonstration of a method. Analysis of place names in English or Welsh allows emendation of (for example) 'Badon' or 'Degsastan', which make no sense, to names that do make sense and can be found on the map. The technique can be applied to sites other than battlefields. The sixth-century writer Gildas refers to the (fourth-century?) martyrdom of Aaron and Julius at 'Legionum urbs', often taken as Caerleon, in south-east Wales. Yet the form is better emended to *Legorum urbs* or Leicester, more important than Caerleon, and hence a likelier place for persecution of Christians. Again, for St Patrick, who refers to his home at the obscure 'Bannaventa Burniae', it is not difficult to show this (after Ludwig Bieler and the local historian Harry Jelley) as a corruption of *Bannaventa Tabernae* (Bannaventa of the Tavern) and therefore Banwell, Avon. St Patrick would have been a Somerset man, living near the opulence of Roman Bath, but also near a low-lying coast dangerously open to Irish predators.

This does not limit the applications of place names. If *British Battles 493–937* demonstrates their significance for military history, three volumes in preparation show their uses elsewhere. My 'England's Earliest Woman Writer and Other Studies on Dark Age Christianity' presents new evidence on monastic sites in Celtic Britain and beyond, including a previously unknown school of learning at Old Kea, near Truro. Recorded as a mysterious 'Rosnat', it was an embryo Celtic university, attracting students from sixth-century Ireland and Wales, who there made intensive study of the Bible. 'The Arthur of History and Other Arthurian Studies' sets out the career of Arthur, a Strathclyde general (the 'King Arthur' of legend) killed in 537 at *Camlan* or Castlesteads on Hadrian's Wall (as argued below). It then moves on to Arthurian tradition and the Cheshire magnate Sir John Stanley (d. 1414), author (it seems) of the Arthurian romance *Sir Gawain and the Green Knight*, the poem's references to Welsh and border places being among the clues for this. Finally, 'Place-Names of Roman Britain: Studies and a Dictionary' will contain new etymologies for ancient toponyms, with those of Cirencester, Doncaster, Kent, London, Manchester, Richborough, Salisbury, Severn, Trent, Wharfe, Wroxeter and York among them. Like the present volume, these books make findings on Britain's early languages widely available, so that much of what is mysterious in Britain's past can be brought to light.

If so, it is in part owing to those who gave assistance over the years by sending information, books, offprints or invitations to publish, and whom I thank here: Rosamund Allen, Martin Aurell, Wayne Barham, Carole Biggam, Tim Clarkson, Iestyn Daniel, Ken Dark, David Dumville, Piero Favero, Marged Haycock, Nicholas Higham, Carole Hough, Christopher Howse, Nicolas Jacobs, Kurt Liebhard, Brian Murdoch, Leonard Neidorf, Michiko Ogura, Donncha Ó hAodha, Brynley F. Roberts, Jane Roberts, Hans Sauer, Tom Shippey, Michael Swanton and Nikolai Tolstoy. I owe them much. But to those mentioned in the dedication to this volume, naturally, I owe far more.

A map of the battlefields is discussed in this book. Original topographic map © Equestenebrarum, via Wikimedia Commons, licensed under the Creative Commons Attribution 3.0 Unported license (http://creativecommons.org/licenses/by/3.0/deed.en).

Chapter 1

493: BRITISH TRIUMPH AT MOUNT BADON OR BRAYDON, WILTSHIRE

We begin this chronicle of slaughter and fighting men by discussing a battle in Wiltshire. It is a county which (fortunately) has seen few conflicts, despite its central position. In the spring or summer of 493 it was yet the location of *Mons Badonicus* or Mount Badon, described by the British historian Gildas, writing in 536. Even though this British victory halted Anglo-Saxon conquests for half a century, there has been no agreement on its date or location, despite a hazy belief in the former as between 490 and 520, and in the latter as in north Wiltshire, perhaps near Badbury, south of Swindon. Also unsure is whether the leader of the Britons was Arthur or Ambrosius Aurelianus. If we could be certain on these points, knowledge of Britain's history would progress considerably.

In what follows, six conclusions are offered: (a) Gildas wrote in 536, as argued in 2010 by David Woods of Cork; (b) the Siege of Mount Badon was 43 years earlier, and so in 493; (c) obscure and meaningless 'Badon' is a scribal error, and must be corrected to *Braydon*; (d) the siege was thus at Ringsbury, a hillfort above Braydon Forest, near Swindon; (e) Arthur, a North British warrior killed in 537, had no connection with the events in 493; and (f) the general who defeated a West Saxon army (surely marching on Cirencester) was instead the Ambrosius Aurelianus praised by Gildas. These conclusions have been in print for some years, but remain disputed. Hence this book.

An outline of earlier discussion allows understanding of both the problem and the solutions to it. Statements go back a long way. John Leland (d. 1552) quoted one from the twelfth-century chronicler Ralph of Diceto: 'Gildas Britonum gesta flebili sermone descripsit anno domini DLXXXIII' and thus 'sub Mauricio imperatore'.[1] Maurice was Emperor of Byzantium in 582–602, which is far too late. If, however, we knew Ralph's source, it might be of great value; for emended DXXXVI would put Gildas in 536 and Badon in 493, as maintained here.

---

[1] Leland 1774, III, 83.

The difficulties are made clear by Philip Perry (1720–1774), rector of the English College, Valladolid. In a manuscript history (published only recently) he described Gildas as 'born in the year of the Battle of Bannesdowne in 493, forty-four years after the arrival of the Saxons in Britain; or in 520, according to others who place the battle of Bannesdowne to that year', with Perry opting for 493.[2] His choice of 493 can be seen as correct. It thereby contrasts with the vagueness or the misplaced confidence of present-day writers.

In the nineteenth century came progress thanks to an edition of the Welsh annals. The entry for 516 there reads: 'Bellum Badonis, in quo Arthur portavit crucem Domini nostri Jesu Christi tribus diebus et tribus noctibus in humeros suos, et Britones victores fuerint', which (despite the fabulous detail of Arthur's carrying a cross) allows certainty on three things.[3] The Britons triumphed; the form 'Badon', resembling nothing in Celtic, is corrupt; it hence surely derives from Gildas's 'Badonicus', also meaningless and corrupt. Nor can the date 516 be right. It was yet accepted by early historians, declaring how 'the British victory at the Mons Badonicus (AD 516 or 520) stops Saxon progress in this quarter for some fifty years', the 'quarter' being southern England 'to the Avon on the borders of Wilts and Dorset'.[4]

The difficulties as regards 516 were explained by Charles Plummer. Bede gives 449 as the year of *Adventus Saxonum* and Badon as occurring 44 years after that (and so in 493). Plummer, thinking Gildas more likely to be writing in 493 + 44 = 537 than in 516 + 44 = 560, preferred 493 to 516. The double sequence of some 44 years he regarded as 'mere coincidence'.[5] On Badon, Plummer thus chose 493, not 516. Sir John Lloyd further remarked on how 'the battle of Badon Hill, fought about the year 500, was a decisive victory for the Britons, giving them immunity from hostile attack for a generation'; not until '550 or thereabouts' did English attacks on the Britons start again.[6] Hugh Williams also considered Badon as occurring 'shortly before or shortly after 500'.[7] John Lloyd-Jones provided Welsh-language references to Badon, none of them in early sources.[8] That total lack of allusion to a British victory is singular. It implies that the Welsh knew of it almost solely from Gildas. This undermines any link between Badon and Arthur. The battle evidently formed no part of native bardic tradition – remarkable, because it was a

---

[2] Carrera and Carrera 2009, 146.
[3] Williams ab Ithel 1860, 4.
[4] Haddan and Stubbs 1869–78, I, 43.
[5] Plummer 1896, II, 30–31.
[6] Lloyd 1911, 125, 127.
[7] Williams 1912, 350.
[8] Lloyd-Jones 1931–63, 49.

British triumph; double remarkable, because some will have it that the victorious troops were led by Arthur himself.

Convenient maps for non-archaeologists were supplied by William Rees. The impression is of English settlements clustering around Oxford, against a blank around Cirencester.[9] It may be taken with comments by Kenneth Jackson. He regarded the victory of Badon as 'approximately round the year 500. The site of the battle is unknown, though Badbury Hill above the Vale of White Horse and Badbury near Swindon are possible candidates. In any case the enemy was evidently the Saxon warriors of the South-East.'[10] Jackson's advocacy of Badbury near Swindon is close to the arguments for Braydon given below. He later said this. Although 'the exact date has been much disputed, it must have been not far from 500. This suits remarkably the known history of southern England, from which it appears that the Anglo-Saxon penetration of the south-east during the first half-century of the invasion was stopped about 500, when it had reached the borders of Salisbury Plain in Berkshire and Hampshire, and was not resumed until another half-century later. Mount Badon must be somewhere in this area' as being 'evidently somewhere in Wessex.'[11]

The 1960s saw little fundamental change. Count Tolstoy, in an ingenious account, argues that the 'Badon was fought in the forty-fourth year' after Ambrosius. Since he places the Battle of *Guoloph* or Wallop (in west Hampshire) in 458, that puts Badon in 501, and even 'on Friday, 29 January 501'.[12] But Gildas did not write as late as 544. An official archaeological map shows more pagan burials in the Winchester and Salisbury regions than were indicated by Rees in 1951. It also represents Roman roads and prehistoric trackways.[13] Precise dating of those burials may indicate whether an attack in 493 was more likely to come from Abingdon and Dorchester-on-Thames, or else Winchester, or these places combined.

Sheppard Frere summed up the then orthodoxy in careful words. 'A long period of fluctuating warfare culminated at some date rather before 500 than after in a British victory at Mount Badon, an unidentified site perhaps in the south-west; after it there was peace for two generations. Gildas, writing soon after 540, is able to speak of "our present security" and of a generation which had no experience of the great struggle.'[14] Bishop Hanson had a slightly

---

[9] Rees 1951, plates 18, 19.
[10] Jackson 1953, 199.
[11] Jackson 1959a, 2, 4.
[12] Tolstoy 1960–62, 149–54.
[13] *Map of Britain* 1966.
[14] Frere 1967, 382–83.

different angle. After acerbic comments on speculations by Nora Chadwick and (especially) John Morris, he nevertheless took the Saxons as conquering up to the Solent but thereafter being 'driven back and contained by the action of Ambrosius, and perhaps of Arthur'. The final victory of Mons Badonis located by some at Badbury Rings in Dorset 'is assigned by all the authorities to about the year 500'.[15] Similar is the statement (after Stenton) on how the date, 'judging by all available evidence, is believed to be about AD 500'.[16]

An interesting challenge to orthodoxy then came from Leslie Alcock. He accepted that 516 CE in the annals is impossible for Badon if Maelgwn (a Gwynedd ruler denounced by Gildas) died in 547 and it took place 43 years before the time of writing. There is a further difficulty. A Welsh-Latin document 'dates the conflict of Ambrosius and Vitolinus, *Catguoloph*, to 437. If Ambrosius was already an eminent general by that date, it is unlikely that he saw active service after 475', while other considerations led Alcock to favour 490 CE for Badon.[17] The problem is best resolved by relating the conflict of 437 (which was certainly at Wallop, near the Roman road from Winchester to Salisbury) not to Ambrosius Aurelianus but to his father, as implied by Gildas's comments on the family's status.

Rightly taking Arthur as a Northerner, and Mount Badon as in south Britain (with a swipe at the 'Somerset, with its mythical "Camelot"' of Leslie Alcock), Charles Thomas followed John Morris on the battle as of about 500 CE.[18] In a posthumous book, Morris spoke of British victory in 'the 490s, a few years on either side of 495', which is true; of the English coming 'to besiege Arthur on Badon Hill, near Bath', which is false; and of Arthur himself as an 'emperor' fighting campaigns throughout Britain, which is fantasy.[19] Ian Wood here performed a dramatic telescoping of events, with Gildas writing at the very time of the engagement, the 43 years being the time-lapse since the victory of Ambrosius in another conflict. 'At the earliest the *De Excidio* would belong to the last fifteen years of the fifth century, at the latest to the 520s.'[20] But nobody has accepted this.

Writing in his mid-80s, Myres repeated views on Badon expressed 50 years previously, still putting it no 'earlier than 490 or later than 516'.[21] Wallace-Hadrill, with judicial astuteness, observed that while Bede dated Badon to

---

[15] Hanson 1968, 19.
[16] Colgrave and Mynors 1969, 54.
[17] Alcock 1971, 53–54, 110–11.
[18] Thomas 1981, 251.
[19] Morris 1982, 332, 338.
[20] Wood 1984, 23.
[21] Myres 1986, 226–27.

494–501, 'Gildas would have placed it *c.* 500'; citing Charles-Edwards and Molly Miller, he rejected Ian Wood's translation of Gildas.[22] Oliver Padel has a crucial comment on punctuation. He points out that Gildas's statements on the campaigns of Ambrosius Aurelianus and then on Badon Hill are normally published in separate paragraphs. Yet there is no manuscript justification for this. The passage is a unity, with the implication that 'Mount Badon reads naturally as the victory which crowned the career of Ambrosius Aurelianus himself'.[23] This interpretation accords with evidence for Ambrosius (and his grandsons) as ruling in the Gloucester-Cirencester region, on Wiltshire's borders.

In the 1990s came further remarks from Leslie Alcock. Discussing the political and social status of Cadbury Castle (near Castle Cary, Somerset), he tended to reject Ambrosius as victor at 'the siege of the Badonic Mount' in 'around AD 500'; he also offered an academic *mea culpa*, apologizing (after criticisms by David Dumville and others) for maintaining Arthur's historicity.[24] His retraction was unnecessary. His original belief in Arthur as a British general killed in 537 can be given belated rehabilitation. This Arthur of history yet had no link with Badon, Cadbury, Gildas or South Britain. The victor at Badon was surely Ambrosius Aurelianus.

Following Alcock's capitulation, writers in the twenty-first century have been wary about answering any of these questions, declaring how 'lack of clear evidence of chronology, the absence of a date of composition, and the poverty of place-names and personal names, all leave Gildas's text very much hanging in space and time, and open to a multiplicity of different interpretations'.[25] With the reading 'Badonici montis', Crépin gave the date as 'vers 495' and the battlefield as 'non-identifié'.[26] Karen George nevertheless tried to place *De Excidio*, in about 540, preferring 470–485 for 'the British recovery under Ambrosius', whom she dissociates from Badon, with Gildas writing in 510–530.[27]

Then came an epoch-making paper by David Woods of Cork. It deserves careful attention and has been largely ignored. Woods cites a curious phrase in chapter 93 of *De Excidio*, on a 'certain thick mist and black night' which 'sits upon the whole island' of Britain, referring it to the catastrophic amounts of ash emitted in 535 by a volcano in Central America. The result of this

---

[22] Wallace-Hadrill 1988, 25–26, 215–16.

[23] Padel 1994, 17.

[24] Alcock 1995, 6, 150.

[25] Higham 2002, 57.

[26] Crépin and Lapidge 2005a, 170.

[27] George 2009, 4.

mega-eruption was a cloud which in 536–37 covered the Northern Hemisphere, bringing about a volcanic winter and world-wide famine. Woods cites for its effects the historian Procopius, who in the spring of 536 witnessed the cloud from the Mediterranean.[28] It brought disaster as well to Britain and Ireland, with famines referred to in the annals of both countries. Its implications for Gildas are obvious. He alludes to the cloud, but not the harvest failure. The inference is that he wrote in the summer of 536, after the cloud could be seen in Britain, yet before its effects were obvious (which he would certainly have mentioned). If, then, Gildas wrote in 536, Badon would have been fought in the spring or summer of 493, a month before Gildas was born. The date 493 stated by Bede is thereby shown as correct.

Woods's paper has not gained recognition even now. It does not figure in a cautious account of Gildas, whose *De Excidio* is put 'no later than about 545', for it is silent on 'the major epidemic of plague which struck the Roman world in the 540s', which also tends to rule out the period before 530, indicating Badon as in the 480s or 490s.[29] No mention, however, of Woods or the *mortalitas* of famine in the annal for 537, also the year of Arthur's violent death at Camlan (= *Camboglanna* or Castlesteads on Hadrian's Wall, after a suggestion of O. G. S. Crawford). The very opposite of cautious is Guy Halsall. He says this. First, Gildas's work 'is usually dated to *c*. 540', because Maelgwn died in 547. Then: 'It is frequently claimed that he wrote *c*. 540, but this date lacks any solid foundation. Professor Dumville long ago demolished all the external evidence that might support such a date.' We then hear of narrative structure, 'possibly moving Gildas' composition up to half a century earlier than the usual date of *c*. 540'.[30] This lacks any credibility.

Others differ again. In a repaginated reprint, Dr Padel does not speculate, merely putting Gildas in the sixth century and reproducing the Welsh annal for 516.[31] We also now have an updated bibliography of Gildas, which gives his death as in 570 and his birth as before 504, 43 years previous to Maelgwn Gwynedd's demise in 547.[32] Readers seeking material on Gildas further to that cited above should refer to it. In 2015 I argued that *obsessio Badonici montis* (the Siege of Mount Badon) in chapter 23 of Gildas's *De Excidio* was corrupt. The toponym must be Celtic (ruling out Bath, with an English place name) but corresponds to nothing in Welsh or Cornish. Emend to *Bradonici* and it makes sense. Welsh *brad* (treachery) is a known place-name element, as with

---

[28] Woods 2010.
[29] Charles-Edwards 2013, 215–18.
[30] Halsall 2013, 21, 53, 191.
[31] Padel 2013, 3, 8.
[32] Lapidge 2014.

the stream of Nant Brad (notorious for floods or ambushes?) near Trefgarn, Pembrokeshire, and mentioned in the twelfth-century Book of Llandaff. On that basis, a corrected *Bradonicus* (or *Bratonicus*) can be identified as Braydon, Wiltshire, and the *mons* as that of nearby Ringsbury Camp (National Grid Reference (NGR) SU 0786), 10 miles south-south-east of Cirencester. This Iron Age hillfort would, it seems, be the site of the British defeat of West Saxons in the spring or summer of 493, recalled by Gildas 43 years later, in the year 536.[33]

Also in 2015, I (with assistance from Tim Clarkson) published locations for the Twelve Battles of Arthur listed in chapter 56 of *Historia Brittonum*, all of them in southern Scotland or the Borders and datable to 536–37, with one exception. The odd one out is Badon. It is in southern Britain, was fought in 493 and had nothing to do with Arthur.[34] In the following year these arguments were expanded in the light of David Woods's paper of 2010. Arthur's battles would have been at a time of crisis, not merely in Britain, but in the whole Northern Hemisphere. In late 535 took place a mega-eruption, apparently at Ilopango in what is now El Salvador, where it left a crater some 10 miles long near San Salvador, the capital. Clouds of sulphites and ash entered the upper atmosphere, obscuring the sun and bringing about one of the worst volcanic winters known to historians. The year 536 was one without a summer. Harvests failed all over the world. There was disaster even in the Far East, as shown by Chinese chronicles of the time. Irish annals also refer to 'famine' and 'lack of bread'; Welsh ones to a 'great mortality in Britain and Ireland'. In this context, Arthur's engagements would not have been for territory or gold. Nor were they against Anglo-Saxon invaders, at that date still far from North Britain. They would have been for meat and other food, in the best Celtic traditions of cattle-raiding, and they would (it appears) have been against the British peoples of Cumbria and south-east Scotland, who no doubt attempted retaliation.[35] In the next chapter, we shall see how the men of Rheged got their revenge when Arthur was killed in 537 at *Camlan*, not far from Carlisle.

Naturally, all the above is taking time to seep into the awareness of scholars. Nancy Edwards, citing Charles-Edwards but ignoring Woods, hence puts Gildas in 'the second quarter of the sixth century'.[36] Someone who has noticed Woods's paper is Nick Higham. He admits that the dating of Gildas to 536 from his allusion to a reference to a cloud 'over the whole island' of Britain 'perhaps has some merit', but 'is far from conclusive'. Against that

---

[33] Breeze 2015a.
[34] Breeze 2015b.
[35] Breeze 2016b.
[36] Edwards 2017, 390.

I say that Bede independently put Badon in 493; add the 43 years of Gildas's life, and I have 536; his reference to a cloud over the whole of Britain is thus no accident. In 536, everyone in Europe was talking of the sinister change in the skies. On the site of Badon, Higham is still more dismissive. A connection with Braydon is not 'sufficiently compelling to merit support'. (I disagree.) The site may have been a minor one, 'of relevance only to Gildas and his circle, less a mountain than a hillock.' (I agree. The hill of Ringsbury Camp is distinctive but not spectacular. It rises a mere 150 feet above Braydon Forest.) The form *Badon* 'has no obvious root in the Celtic languages.' (I agree. Hence the need for emendation. In Wales are Y Bradnant, Nant Brad, Bratffos and Pant-y-Brad; in Somerset is Bradon. A connection of all these, after a suggestion of Professor Richard Coates, with Welsh *brad* (treachery), and emendation of 'Badonicus' to *Bradonicus*, thus brings meaning to what has none.) By the process of consequent reasoning outlined above, we reject Professor Higham's bluff assertion that we 'would be better off today facing up to the fact that Badon is lost'.[37] Not so. It is there for the finding, if coherent thought and logic are applied to the evidence.

Still more recently, Iestyn Daniel puts the engagement not in 493 or even 516, but in 665.[38] This startling claim he makes on the basis, not of books and articles cited above, but of publications by the Rev. A. W. Wade-Evans (1875–1964) and the local historian J. P. Brown (1926–2008) of Llangollen. It provides a most interesting lesson in historical judgement and the unexpected ways in which our understanding of the past is advanced or retarded. Two points can be made. First, we take Wade-Evans and Brown. Throughout his long career as cleric and scholar, Wade-Evans made the claim that the text of Gildas as we have it is not a unity but consists of two pieces, only one of them written by the writer of the early sixth century. His views never had much hold outside nationalist circles and are dismissed by mainstream scholars, who with reason regard *De Excidio* as a single work. Daniel's renewed advocacy of his views thus brings us back sharply to Welsh nationalist opinion of the 1940s and 1950s (what one might call the glory days of Plaid Cymru) when its ideology owed much to Saunders Lewis (1893–1985), in which greatness and eccentricity (not least on literary history) were so curiously combined. As for Joe Brown, whom I met at Celtic conferences in the 1990s, his work indicates the difficulties of independent scholarship. Some of his research appeared in the Welsh-language newspaper *Y Faner*. Other items, finding no publisher, were bequeathed to the National Library of Wales. They were doomed to have minimal influence until Dr Daniel consulted them.

---

[37] Higham 2018, 156, 192–93.
[38] Daniel 2019, 57–59, 373.

Now, what is said in a later chapter on *Maserfelth* in 642 depends heavily on Joe Brown's investigations on the boundaries of *Meisyr*, as has been made better known by Jenny Rowland. Brown's work is fundamental in establishing the location of this Anglo-Saxon battle, and his memory deserves respect for that. Like others on the fringes of scholarship who are cited in this book, he showed the way ahead (unlike many others). Nevertheless, what is said on Badon and the seventh century and the splitting of *De Excidio* between two authors has no credibility, for this reason. That leads to our other point.

The allusion in *Annales Cambriae* to the second battle of Badon seems puzzling, yet it has a simple explanation, which has already been given in the articles of 2015 that are the foundation for this chapter. Now, the first conflict, between Briton and West Saxon, was in 493 and took place in what is now north Wiltshire. Thanks to the fame of Gildas, it was never forgotten in Celtic-Latin culture (although we have previously observed that the vernacular tradition of bardic poetry and the like knew nothing of it until Geoffrey of Monmouth began producing his forgeries in the 1130s, when it was ultimately given as *Baddon* or Bath). After the fall in 577 of Cirencester, Gloucester and Bath to the English, central southern Britain became well and truly England. All the same, memory of 'Badon' as having been somewhere in the region was still remembered by those who compiled Welsh annals. It provides a solution for that 'second' Battle of Badon in 665; for we know from English chronicles how in 661 the Mercian king Wulfhere, son of Penda, and the dominant force in the south Britain of his day, 'ravaged from Ashdown'. Because Ashdown is the upland region in Berkshire, south of the Vale of White Horse and with an ancient ridgeway leading into Wiltshire, whoever wrote the Welsh-Latin entry for 665 thought of Wulfhere's raids (with the slight misdating frequent in annals of this period) as 'the second battle of Badon'. Once this is understood, the need to put the conflict in Gildas's text at this late date (and to split it into two widely differing portions) must collapse.

We have reached the end of our first part. It will be seen on the dating of Badon that scholars of the twenty-first century are in much the same boat as their predecessors in the eighteenth, sixteenth, twelfth or even eighth centuries. So, then, a second and final part, which is brief, for accounts of Mount Badon can now be accessed from Higham's book of 2018. The argument is simple. Comparison with Welsh toponyms allows the correction of Gildas's meaningless 'Mons Badonicus' to *Mons Bradonicus* (or even *Bratonicus*) and identification with the Iron Age hillfort of Ringsbury above *Braydon* Forest. Attempts by Kenneth Jackson and others to locate the British victory in north Wiltshire will be vindicated. The work of David Woods also puts the engagement in 493 CE, as stated independently by Bede.

It thereby offers (among other things) a task for Wiltshire archaeologists. Ringsbury is in the parish of Purton, known for Roman and Anglo-Saxon remains including 'a small seventh-century cemetery', and so resembling Highworth to the east of it, with 'clear evidence for both Romano-British and early Anglo-Saxon occupation'.[39] Similar archaeological research may confirm that its hillfort was occupied in the late fifth century, as perhaps was the stronghold on Bury Hill (NGR SU 0690) two miles north-north-west of it. If, of course, battle-archaeologists can prove that there is no sign of military activity around 493 in this region, then the case for Badon–Braydon will collapse. A new start would have to be made. Either way, it is good that modern archaeologists are in a position to resolve the problem decisively.

There are also lessons for historians. Whether the Battle of 'Mount Badon' was in north Wiltshire (as I think) or not, its date is certain. If Gildas wrote *De Excidio* in the early summer of 536, the British victory (whatever its location) would have been in 493. It led to 50 years of freedom for the Britons from Anglo-Saxon attack, with permanent effects for (among other things) English toponyms, as shown by the frequency of Celtic place names in (say) Shropshire or Somerset, as against Suffolk or Kent. If archaeological investigation also confirms that the Siege of Mount Badon was in Wiltshire, it will be the most important battle ever fought in the county, and (with its clash of Celt against Saxon) one of the most dramatic battles ever seen in Britain – giving 50 years of respite for the island's dying British-Latin civilization, so that it was ultimately linked (quite wrongly) with the North British champion Arthur.

---

[39] Draper 2011, 97.

Chapter 2

537: ARTHUR'S DEATH AT CAMLAN OR CASTLESTEADS, CUMBRIA

The British hero Arthur has been a headache for scholars. Some maintain that there is no historical evidence for him, and that he is as mythical as Robin Hood or Father Christmas. In what follows, we turn that upside down. Arthur is as historical as Oliver Cromwell or Abraham Lincoln, and we have plenty of hard information on him, including the place and date of his death: in 537 at *Camlan* or Castlesteads, on Hadrian's Wall, north-east of Carlisle. Like his other battles, it belongs to southern Scotland and the Borders. How we reach that solution is the purpose of this chapter.

Authentic knowledge of Arthur comes from three sources: a polemical tract written by Gildas in 536 and mentioning the Battle of Mount Badon of 493; the entry for 537 in *Annales Cambriae;* and a list of 12 battles in the ninth-century *Historia Brittonum,* which includes Badon. We start with the second as edited by John Williams ab Ithel (1811–1862). It reads, 'Gueith Camlann, in qua Arthur et Medraut corruere; et mortalitas in Britannia et Hibernia fuit.'[1] The editor explained *gueith* as Old Welsh for 'battle', while *Camlann* was identified by the archaeologist O. G. S. Crawford (1886–1957) as the fort of *Camboglanna* on Hadrian's Wall. The 'Medraut' who fell with Arthur is otherwise unknown. As for *mortalitas,* it has been translated as 'plague', but it should be taken as 'famine', part of a worldwide one during the volcanic winter of 536–37, the consequence of a volcanic eruption in the Americas, probably at Ilopango in El Salvador. The reasoning for that appears below.

Now for Gildas. There are two references in his work. In the first, after telling how the Britons under Ambrosius Aurelianus resisted Anglo-Saxon aggression, he states in chapter 26 that the struggle went this way and that 'up to the year of the siege of Badon Hill (*obsessionis Badonis montis*)', which was 'also the year of my birth' 43 years and a month prior to the time of writing. The second reference is in chapter 93, where he alludes to 'a certain

---

[1] Williams ab Ithel 1860, 4, 120.

thick mist and black night' sitting 'upon the whole island' of Britain.[2] In 2010 it was referred by Dr David Woods to the cloud of volcanic ash covering the Northern Hemisphere in 536–37. The cloud was witnessed by Procopius (the historian of Byzantium), who described how for months 'the sun shone like the moon, without its rays, very much as if in an eclipse'. Because Gildas says nothing on the famine produced by the cloud, we infer that (a) he wrote in the summer of 536, after the sun became obscured, but before harvests failed and people began to starve; (b) the battle at Mount Badon occurred 43 years and a month previous, and therefore in the spring or summer of 493, when Gildas was born; and (c) Arthur took no part in the conflict.

The third item on the Arthur of history is a catalogue of 12 battles in *Historia Brittonum*. It was treated with respect by Gibbon. Relying on its 'simple and circumstantial testimony', he declared how according to this, 'the most rational account', Arthur 'defeated, in twelve successive battles, the Angles of the North and the Saxons of the West'. He yet observed how, after 'the light of science and reason was rekindled' in modern times, doubts on Arthur grew to the point that 'by a natural, though unjust, reverse of the public opinion, the severity of the present age is inclined to question the *existence* of Arthur.'[3] By use of the Welsh language (to which he confessed himself 'a stranger'), we shall vindicate Gibbon, who rightly believed in the Arthur of history.

To do that we begin with some toponyms set out by William Watson (1865–1948), for many years Professor of Celtic at Edinburgh. They are the names of Pennango, south of Hawick; Dreva, on the Tweed west of Peebles; Karig Lion, near Kinneil, West Lothian; Carstairs, near Lanark; Tarras Water in the east of Dumfries and Galloway; and Douglas Water, near Lanark.[4] These can all be related to chapter 56 of *Historia Brittonum*. With Arthur's battles there presented as against Anglo-Saxons in Kent, the passage gives the first engagement as at the mouth of a river called 'Glein'; the second, third, fourth, and fifth on the river 'Dubglas' in the region of 'Linnuis'; the sixth on the river 'Bassas'; the seventh in the forest of 'Celidon'; the eighth at the fortress of 'Guinnion'; the ninth at the 'City of the Legion' (in urbe Legionis); the tenth on a river-bank called 'Tribruit'; the eleventh by a hill called 'Agned'; and the twelfth and greatest at Mount Badon (in monte Badonis).[5]

Four of these can be identified at once. 'Bassas' making no sense in Celtic, we emend to *Tarras*. There are or were two rivers of this name. It was formerly used of Mouse Water near Car*stairs* (which preserves the form): it is still the

---

[2] Williams 1899–1901, 60–63, 217.
[3] Gibbon 1904, 130–31.
[4] Watson 1926, 354, 363, 383–84, 386–87, 457–58.
[5] Chambers 1927, 239.

name of Tarras Water in Eskdale, further south, near the border with Cumbria. Unfortunately, which of the two marked the battlefield cannot be decided, but they still put Arthur in southern Scotland. Clearer is the 'City of the Legion'. It has been taken as Chester or Caerleon, where the form translates Old Welsh or Cumbric *cair lion*. There being no reason to place Arthur anywhere near the border of modern Wales, it is better taken as a corruption of *Karig Lion* (cliff of (the) legion) at the east end of the Antonine Wall, in Lothian. The Welsh scribes who transmitted the text of the passage had never heard of this obscure place overlooking the Firth of Forth, and naturally substituted for its name that of cities nearer to Wales, which they did know about. As for Tribruit, a Celtic form meaning 'speckled (river-bank)', it will be Dreva, on the Upper Tweed, where an English etymology can be ruled out. 'Agned' being meaningless as it stands, we emend to Old Welsh *agheu* meaning 'death'. That 'hill of death' would have been *Penanngo*, Borders. Thanks to Watson, four of the battlefields can thus be pinpointed to within Scotland.

To them, the four engagements on the River Douglas in 'Linnuis' can be added. Linnuis is often taken as Lindsey or north Lincolnshire. But Lincolnshire has no River Douglas. Emend 'Linnuis' to Old Welsh *Cluduis* 'Strathclyders, people on the River Clyde', which Douglas Water flows into, and the expression makes sense. *Cludwys*, in Middle Welsh spelling, was known to the bards, like *Camlan* itself.[6] Welsh poets knew of *Camlan*, where Arthur fell, and of the realm of *Cludwys* 'Strathclyders'. Yet they knew nothing of Arthur at Badon until they heard of it from Geoffrey of Monmouth, a literary forger. We can be certain that Arthur died in 537 at Camlan on the Roman Wall, but had no part in the British triumph in 493 at 'Badon' in north Wiltshire.

While we take in the implications here, a note on the source of *Historia Brittonum*'s passage. The Chadwicks thought that the chronicler's source was 'in all probability to be sought in a catalogue poem' resembling ones in early Welsh. They added that 'Mons Badonis is not likely to have been in the north'.[7] Following the Chadwicks, we take the 'Glein' as the River Glen of north Northumberland.[8] The outlines of our argument are already clear. Of the 12 battles, 10 have been located: 8 in southern Scotland, 1 in Northumberland and 1 in Wiltshire. Yet 'Badon', as noted, had no connection with Arthur.

As for *Camlan* in the Welsh annals, Robin Collingwood (1889–1943) regarded Crawford's 1935 proposal that Camlan was *Camboglanna* on Hadrian's Wall as convincing. (The fort was previously taken as Birdoswald, but is now thought to be Castlesteads, nearer to Carlisle.) Collingwood further declared that

---

[6] Lloyd-Jones 1931–63, 49, 101, 149.
[7] Chadwick and Chadwick 1932, 154–55, 162.
[8] Ekwall 1936, 58–59, 189.

Arthur was 'not a king, still less king over all the kings of Britain'. Not good, however, was his acceptance of the *Historia Brittonum* catalogue as indicating places up and down the island. Out of them he constructed an elaborate myth of Arthur as 'last of the Romans', having a commission 'valid all over the country' and a command over 'a mobile field army', perhaps consisting of 'heavy cavalry, clothed in chain mail'.[9] Appearing in the Oxford History of England, his conjectures were influential.

Kenneth Jackson (1909–1991) of Edinburgh was sceptical. On whether Arthur was a 'leader of the Roman kind' as argued by Collingwood, or a mere tyrant like Vortigern, he thought that 'nothing useful can be said'. As for Mount Badon, which he placed in or near north Wiltshire, with 'the enemy evidently the Saxons of the south-east', he said merely that Arthur 'may or may not have been' the victor.[10] Different views came from his pupil Rachel Bromwich (1915–2010), who consistently took Arthur as 'a heroic figure of the North', the obscure names of *Historia Brittonum* perhaps concealing 'corrupt forms of place-names within the northern area'.[11] Jackson's reply was prompt. Against those arguing for the 12 battles as northern ones, he riposted that 'the philological evidence relied on by the proponents of this view does little to support it'.[12] Yet there can be no doubt here that Rachel Bromwich was right.

Now for Sir Winston Churchill. Despite an understandable tendency to make out Arthur as (like himself) a defender of civilization against barbarism, he displayed shrewdness and a grip on reality in his observations. Commenting on those who even in his time said, 'No Arthur; at least, no proof of any Arthur', he was pithy. If the 'knights in steel' and 'bewitching ladies' enshrined 'in a glorious circle lit by victory' are nothing but the 'invention of a Welsh writer', then 'he must have been a marvellous inventor'. Churchill also remarked on how some historians, out of 'fear of being contradicted', strip themselves 'of almost all sense and meaning'. After quoting one such writer (unnamed), he pronounced a gruff verdict: 'That is not much to show after so much toil and learning.' But Churchill was the last man to admit defeat. 'It is all true, or it ought to be; and more and better besides.' Despite yielding to Collingwood's interpretation of Arthur as commanding fast-moving troops, Churchill demonstrated his grasp of strategy by accepting Mount Badon as in the 'Debatable Lands' near Swindon and its date as between 490 and 503.[13] Like Gibbon, Churchill defended the historical Arthur.

---

[9] Collingwood and Myres 1937, 320–24.
[10] Jackson 1953, 116, 199.
[11] Bromwich 1954, 83–136.
[12] Jackson 1955, 77–88.
[13] Churchill 1956, 46–48.

In a discussion which remains essential, Kenneth Jackson was non-committal.[14] He did not know whether Arthur existed, although 'he may well have existed', the nature of the evidence being such that 'proof is impossible'. He made further observations. *Arthur* is 'unquestionably derived from *Artorius*', so that the hero had a name of Latin origin. Mount Badon is in southern England, perhaps in Wiltshire, Berkshire or Dorset. Jackson also noted 'Arthur' as a name given to North British princes in the late sixth century. He then gave an account of the Twelve Battles. Mount Badon is 'in Wessex'; the 'City of the Legion' is 'certainly Chester'; the Caledonian Forest is 'somewhere in Strathclyde'. The four battles on an 'unidentified river *Dubglas*' were probably in Lincolnshire. Jackson made an interesting observation on *Mons Breguoin*, substituted in *Historia Brittonum*'s 'Vatican Recension' (of 944) for *Mons Agned*. He took *Breguoin* as the Roman fort of *Bremenium* or High Rochester, Northumberland, if admitting that the form 'may be an interpolation'. (It is. But it shows a tenth-century scholar regarding Arthur as a Northerner, not a Welshman or Cornishman. Hence his locating it within 20 miles of 'Mons Agned', which can be emended to *Agheu* and placed at *Pennango*, south of Hawick.) For the rest of the 11, Jackson located the engagement on the River Glen as in Northumberland or Lincolnshire, 'but this is highly uncertain. The remainder are entirely unknown.' On Camlan in *Annales Cambriae*, he still regarded Crawford's suggestion of *Camboglanna* on Hadrian's Wall as 'ingenious and by no means impossible'.

So much for Jackson in 1959. On the 12 battles, Count Tolstoy provided an exhaustive survey. On the Caledonian Forest he has a useful quotation from Hector Boece (d. 1536) for it as the area north of Moffat in the Southern Uplands, in the wild country around Beattock Summit.[15] Echoing Collingwood, Sheppard Frere thereafter spoke of Arthur as the 'victor of Mount Badon' who 'succeeded Ambrosius in the leadership' and who with 'some sort of unified command arranged between petty kingdoms' led 'mounted forces' to 'strike back at the Saxons'.[16] For contrary views we turn to Bishop Hanson (1916–1988) and Kenneth Jackson. Hanson showed scant respect for academic opinions, especially those of John Morris. He observed how Nora Chadwick considered that, if Arthur did exist, 'it was in north Britain, whence his legend has been transferred to Wales and Cornwall'; her husband H. M. Chadwick (1870–1947), on the other hand, had associated Arthur with rulers of Devon and Cornwall, thinking that Arthur was born in south-west Britain between 450 and 470, and 'took part in the battle of *Mons Badonis*, 490–500'.[17] As for

---

[14] Jackson 1959, 1–11.
[15] Tolstoy 1960–62, 118–62.
[16] Frere 1967, 382.
[17] Hanson 1968, 20.

Jackson, he gave a warning in characteristic tones. 'It has become a favourite dogma amongst some writers that the British peoples in the Dark Ages had a great military organization like a sort of Horse Guards or Dragoons, and that in particular this is true of King Arthur.' Jackson attributed this to 'the romantic and eloquent' theories of Collingwood. Unfortunately, 'there is not the slightest real evidence that Arthur, if he ever existed, had anything to do with cavalry.' After other remarks, he yet concluded on how 'no doubt we shall see characters in Welsh Dark Age tradition claimed as "Roman cavalry officers" for a long time to come'. Elsewhere he remarked of an obscure allusion to Arthur in Aneirin's *Gododdin* that, because 'Arthur was the great national hero of the entire British people, from Scotland to Brittany', there is 'no logic whatever in the idea that this reference can be used to support the theory that he was a Northern leader'.[18]

In the 1970s there was apotheosis of Arthur as British hero or even emperor. Some of this was a result of Leslie Alcock's excavations at Cadbury Castle, Somerset. Alcock's best-known book had extensive speculation on Arthur, including a map of his battles at sites from the Highlands of Scotland to Dorset. One engagement, that of Badon, is put at no fewer than six possible places.[19] In the same year came Stenton's scrupulous observation on how Gildas's silence 'may suggest that the Arthur of history was a less imposing figure than the Arthur of legend'.[20] We modify this, proposing Arthur as a figure who gained fame only in 536, when Gildas was actually writing. Another archaeologist, Charles Thomas (1928–2016), published comments on Arthur which were well informed, thanks to the use of a paper by Thomas Jones (1910–1972) of Aberystwyth. Thomas felt sure that Arthur existed and that early references to him 'take us firmly to North Britain'.[21] For Somerset, although Leslie Alcock in a section headed 'Cadbury and Arthur' admitted that 'no personal relic' of the British hero 'was found during the excavations there', the stronghold was still 'a suitable base' for the thousand or so men who would be under Arthur's command.[22]

It was with John Morris's *Age of Arthur* that the high-point of invention was reached, with considerable learning, remarkable insights and a legion of wild ideas. As a sample of the last, his words on Camlan. Its site is unknown. 'But, whatever the place and cause of the battle, the result was catastrophic. With Arthur died the unity of Britain, and all hope of reviving it under British

---

[18] Jackson 1969, 85–86, 112.
[19] Alcock 1971, 62.
[20] Stenton 1971, 3.
[21] Thomas 1971, 39.
[22] Alcock 1972, 193.

rule.'[23] Reaction was swift. Professor Dumville pricked the bubble of Morris's imaginings to such effect that almost all professional scholars now think Arthur an illusion.[24] The obscurity of his battles was such that D. Simon Evans (1921–1998) of Lampeter confessed that it was hard to locate any of them: 'nid hawdd nabod y lleoedd a olygir'.[25] Becoming no subject for historians, Arthur was (with logic) ignored by many. The attack came too late to be cited in Rachel Bromwich's guide to Welsh tradition.[26] But it was taken up by others. There is a start with comments on how 'Arthur's existence' and still more 'his position as one of the greatest war-leaders of his day' are 'a matter of dispute'.[27] In the midst of this appeared Morris's posthumous handbook of Arthurian sources, with remarks on the battle catalogue as demonstrating how 'before Badon, the campaign that was regarded as most important was fought in Lincolnshire' (it also mistranslates *mortalitas* in the annal for 537 as 'plague').[28]

How the work of Alcock and Morris gained ground and then lost it was shown by Peter Salway. In his main text he speaks of 'a growing movement to believe in the historicity of Arthur' as victor at Mount Badon and with Cadbury Castle as his 'Camelot', if with the rider that the question must be 'held in abeyance' until the texts were properly examined by qualified specialists. In a postscript is comment on Dumville's 1977 paper, leaving the author as 'even less confident about the course of events in fifth-century Britain than before'.[29] We shall hear more on those lines. In 1971 Charles Thomas had believed in Arthur and spoken of how the references 'take us firmly to North Britain'. Ten years later he had changed sides. He wrote words which may be too memorable. 'Many will agree with David Dumville's *cri de coeur*: "The fact of the matter is that there is no historical evidence about Arthur; we must reject him from our histories and, above all, from the titles of our books." Any sane person would agree.' He added that 'it may be preferable, and in the particular case of Arthur it is *desirable*, to construct models of fifth-century Britain devoid of individual names altogether.'[30] From Oxford came terser comments. The sources for Arthur are meagre and 'unlikely to derive from contemporary materials. That is all. And on that little all the imagination of the learned and unlearned has run riot'. With such words 'the inexhaustible,

---

[23] Morris 1973, 140.
[24] Dumville 1977, 173–92.
[25] Evans 1977, 70.
[26] Bromwich 1978, 274–77, 544–45.
[27] Johnson 1980, 123.
[28] Morris 1980, 5, 35, 45, 85.
[29] Salway 1981, 485, 501.
[30] Thomas 1981, 245.

if rather ridiculous, interest in trying to work out who the "real" Arthur was' is put aside.[31]

Unnoticed here was a bleak statement '536: Famine' in an Oxford history of Ireland.[32] It proves that the *mortalitas* in Britain and Ireland recorded by the Welsh annal for 537 was not plague but starvation, following extreme weather conditions that are known of from other sources. Then came a voice from the grave. John Morris's final book tells how 'Arthur's empire set about the recovery of the whole of the former Roman diocese, to the farthest limits that Roman rule had ever reached', with wars in the Scottish Highlands and against barbarians in South Wales. It concludes on how 'the personal prestige of Badon kept Arthur's empire in being for twenty years', until disaster came at Camlan. 'Like the successors of Alexander of Macedonia eight centuries before, the generals fought each other when the enemy was defeated, and the founder of the empire left no heir.'[33]

Moving to other writers, we encounter Professor Lapidge as editor, with complex attempts to date Gildas.[34] Reissuing what he wrote in the 1930s, J. N. L. Myres said nothing new on Badon. But he had plenty to say on Morris. Dismissing the title of *The Age of Arthur* as showing 'total disregard of the valid historical evidence', he likewise cast Arthur into outer darkness, there being 'no contemporary or near-contemporary evidence' for him as a shaper of events. No such figure 'has wasted more of the historian's time'.[35] In calmer terms, Wallace-Hadrill quoted Charles Thomas on how 'in the particular case of "Arthur" it is *desirable* to construct models of fifth-century Britain devoid of individual names'; he also cited attempts to date Badon, including Bede's indication of the early 490s.[36]

There is more negativism from editors of an eleventh-century Arthurian text, who declared that the site of Camlan (crooked bank) is 'impossible to determine', because there are 'many other "crooked banks" to be found throughout Britain'.[37] These objections did not occur to them: that *Camboglanna*, as a fort on the Roman Wall, had a military significance denied to other 'crooked banks'; that it is in the North, like known battlefields of Arthur; that nothing associates the conflict with Wales; and that if it had been in Wales, it is unlikely that the site of such a disaster would be forgotten. The

---

[31] Campbell 1982, 20–44.
[32] Moody, Martin, and Byrne 1982, 19.
[33] Morris 1982, 341, 343.
[34] Dumville 1984, 51–59.
[35] Myres 1986, 15–16.
[36] Wallace-Hadrill 1988, 21, 214–16.
[37] Bromwich and Evans 1992, 84–85.

ascendancy of the anti-Arthurians still continued. Ken Dark, in a study of British political continuity from 300 to 800, never mentions Arthur at all.[38] It also had results for Leslie Alcock. He made submission in his final book on the Cadbury Castle digs, saying this. Within 'the scholarly framework of the 1950s and 1960s, the Arthur/Camelot attribution seemed a reasonable inference. The sustained minimalist criticism of the historicity of Arthur was only launched publicly in the late 1970s', where he cites Dumville's paper of 1977, although Alcock adds that he himself had 'rejected the historicity of Camelot by 1969'.[39] But time plays tricks. If Arthur was a fighting man of the 530s, Alcock's publications can be rehabilitated. Archaeologists will look at them with new eyes, especially regarding the Britons of Southern Scotland.

When Arthur was dealt with, it was negatively, as by Dr Oliver Padel. He made determined efforts to dispose of Arthur. Here is an instance. Dr Padel cannot locate the Twelve Battles, but still regards them as showing 'the literary accretion to the name of Arthur of the credit for various famous battles from the distant past'. To this we reply that (Badon excepted) the battles were not 'famous' but obscure. That indicates an authentic tradition. The corruption of their manuscript forms underlines this. Even early scribes did not know where these 'famous' engagements were. Dr Padel nevertheless ends as an anti-Arthurian, asserting that 'it is unnecessary to postulate a historical person behind the legend', with the hero being 'primarily a pan-Brittonic figure of local wonder-tales'.[40] This despite the facts of Arthur's name being Latin (from *Artorius*), and of circumstantial details on his victories, which no forger would invent.

A handbook on pre-Norman England marks the nadir of Arthurianism. He is 'legendary'; he was thought to have led 'British resistance against the Germanic invaders'; battles attributed to him 'cannot be identified', the list probably representing 'the accumulation of legend'; and the entry on his death at Camlan in 537 has 'little or no historical value for the sixth century'.[41] Yet Ken Dark gave comfort to Arthurians in a study of Northern and other princes who in the late sixth century were called after their hero.[42] The phenomenon, which anti-Arthurians cannot explain, points to Arthur as a recent Northern warrior so admired that princes were given his name, an uncommon Latin one.

---

[38] Dark 1994, 258–69.
[39] Alcock 1995, 6.
[40] Padel 1997, 1–31.
[41] Padel 1999.
[42] Dark 2000, 77–95.

In the early twenty-first century, Nick Higham's book on Arthur had much of interest, most of it sceptical. With the exception of the 'City of the Legion' (Chester? Caerleon?), 'Wood of Caledonia' (Strathclyde?), and *Linnuis* (Lindsey?), the Twelve Battles 'are unlocated and, at present, unlocatable'. Crawford's view of Camlan as *Camboglanna* on the Wall 'should probably be set aside as coincidental' because John Koch of Aberystwyth considers the annal for 537 as not 'of any great antiquity in the mid-tenth century'; so 'the whole story is best set aside as unverifiable, and potentially, at least, entirely unhistorical'.[43] Identification of *Camboglanna* with Castlesteads appears in the English Place-Name Society's dictionary, which also describes the Camlan of 'the older Welsh annals' as 'unlocated'.[44]

Later publications for the period thus say little on Arthur or even ignore him. A survey of opinions on Cadbury informs us about Leland's successors, but is questionable on place names, as in relating Cadbury to 'Cadan' on the Hereford Map (where Cadnam in the New Forest seems more likely).[45] Professor Aurell of Poitiers echoes Higham by typifying the conflicts as 'tous ou la plupart, inventés pas l'auteur' or 'plus vraisemblement, empruntés à la tradition des bardes'.[46] A British Archaeological Report on Dark Age Scotland has value for future work on Arthur, particularly on the monumental inscriptions which are almost the sole evidence for Scotland in about 500. They prove that the North Britons were Christians and (at least among the élite) spoke Latin in addition to writing it. Their epigraphy indicates an unexpectedly high standard of 'Latinity and literacy'.[47] No surprise if their greatest hero, Arthur, had a Latin name. James Fraser mentions Dumville's researches on *Historia Brittonum*, but not Arthur.[48] Dr George does not mention him either, yet puts Badon between about 470 and 485, with Gildas writing between about 510 and 530. She also quotes, without comment, the passage on the 'dense cloud and black night' of sin looming 'over the whole island', diverting men 'from the straight way (*via recta*)' into 'trackless and entangled paths of crime'.[49]

For many writers on *Historia Brittonum*, attention shifted from dating the events or locating places in the text to speculation on why it was written. Here Tim Clarkson of Manchester cites Professor Dumville.[50] So does Karen Jankulak, adding that the whereabouts of Camlan, 'like that of all Arthur's

[43] Higham 2002, 146, 208–209.
[44] Watts 2004, 111, 112.
[45] Evans 2006, 226–53.
[46] Aurell 2007, 84.
[47] Forsyth 2009, 19–41.
[48] Fraser 2009, 126.
[49] George 2009, 3–4, 92, 177.
[50] Clarkson 2010, 31–32.

purported battles, is obscure'.[51] Kennedy quotes R. W. Hanning's remark of 1966 on *Historia Brittonum* as 'a dangerous text from which to draw conclusions about actual happenings'.[52]

Then came a paper of epoch-making importance by David Woods of Cork.[53] Its message is this. Gildas's words on the dense cloud (*densissima nebula*) and black night (*atraque nox*) that lie heavy over the whole island of Britain (*omni insulae ita incumbit*) are strange. Woods refers them to the volcanic cloud which covered the Northern Hemisphere from the spring of 536 to late 537. It ruined harvests and brought worldwide starvation. Because Gildas speaks of a cloud over Britain, but is silent on the famine that followed it, the implication is clear. He wrote after the skies became obscured in early 536, but before crops failed later that year, an event mentioned by Welsh and Irish annalists alike. Mount Badon will therefore have been in 493, the year of Gildas's birth, 43 years and a month before he wrote. The battle is too early for Arthur, killed at Camlan in 537. Despite publication in an Oxford journal, Woods's paper was for a while overlooked by Nick Higham, who declared of the battle catalogue that 'it seems safest to view this list as historically spurious'.[54]

Our remaining authors are a mix. First is a lavish volume by an Italian endocrinologist. It is financed by UNESCO and comes with a *prefazione* by a former United Nations under-secretary. It has much on Welsh sites, among which it includes Camlan, 'il luogo della battalgia finale in cui re Artù fu sconfitto da suo nipote', which is located near Dinas Mawddwy in south Gwynedd.[55] Thereafter three books of 2013. In a large volume, Professor Charles-Edwards mentions neither Arthur as a historical character nor Camlan.[56] On the *Historia Brittonum* catalogue Guy Halsall says this:

[The] 'locations of all these battles are unknown and unknowable. This is of supreme importance if reading modern pseudo-histories so I'll say it again:

THE LOCATIONS OF ALL THESE BATTLES ARE UNKNOWN AND UNKNOWABLE

The *Historia Brittonum* is a fascinating, infuriating source. It still holds many secrets, doubtless including ones that no-one will ever uncover.'[57]

---

[51] Jankulak 2010, 72.
[52] Kennedy 2010, 790–91.
[53] Woods 2010, 226–34.
[54] Higham 2011, 9–25.
[55] Favero 2012, 178.
[56] Charles-Edwards 2013, 56, 217.
[57] Halsall 2013, 67.

Meanwhile, Dr Padel in a new issue of a book of 2000 (with modified pagin-
ation and updated bibliography) similarly described the battle catalogue as
having little context, so that 'safe identification is impossible for the most part',
although *Bassas* 'recalls Baschurch in the Welsh Marches', while the City of
the Legion may allude to the Battle of Chester. On Camlan, 'there is no way
of telling whether this battle was thought to be located in Wales' or 'further
north' or 'indeed elsewhere'. In short, as 'historical sources the Annals and the
Historia tend to cancel each other out, because of their inconsistencies'; they
are mere 'literary sources' which 'give us a picture of the Arthurian legend
in the ninth and tenth centuries'.[58] A US writer is, however, more positive,
stating that the entry for 537 'has a strong claim for being historical by way
of two factors. First, the terseness and phrasing of the line is similar to other
early entries. It is therefore probably historical in that the event did happen.
As Arthur is named as a leader in this battle in every source that mentions it,
he most reasonably was present there.'[59] These facts cannot be brushed aside.

It is true that bafflement on the battles goes back a long way, which at last
brings us to Henry of Huntingdon, active in the 1150s. He added the passage
from *Historia Brittonum* to the second book of his *Historia Anglorum*, observing
that 'None of these battle-sites can be identified now'. This comment of the
1150s, quoted in 2015 without remark, demonstrates how English historiog-
raphy made no progress over nine centuries.[60] Nor is Wales better off. Dr
Morgan of Aberystwyth asked of Arthur, 'Where did he fight his greatest
battle, the battle of Mount Badon? Was it near Badbury in Somerset or
Badbury Rings in Dorset, or Mynydd Baedan near Bridgend? As for his last
and fatal battle of Camlan, it is claimed for Hadrian's Wall, for mid-Wales,
for Somerset and for Cornwall. What a puzzle, then, is the figure of Arthur.'[61]
Across the Channel even German scholars shrug their shoulders, with one of
them declaring on Badon that 'there are no historiographical indications that
could allow an exact or even vague dating of this event or the location of it'.[62]

In that same year, however, using material published by Watson in 1926,
I was able to locate all 12 battles, together with a map by Tim Clarkson to
pinpoint them. All, except for Badon, can be placed in Southern Scotland
and the Border, with the clear implication that Arthur was a North Briton.[63]
His account contains Dr Clarkson's own convincing solution on a battle

[58] Padel 2013, 3, 4, 9–10.
[59] Johnson 2014, 17.
[60] Gillingham 2015, 141–56.
[61] Morgan 2015, 133–35.
[62] Schustereder 2015, 77.
[63] Breeze 2015a.

not already located, that of the stronghold called *Guinnion*. He takes it as Carwinning, a hillfort two miles west of Dalry, Ayrshire. His identification is already accepted by a Continental scholar, who gives information on the site, stating that 'Der Hügel hat eine beherrschende Position und war einst von drie konzentrischen Wällen umgeben'. He also (at some expense to himself) reproduces the Ordnance Survey Map of its environs.[64]

Since the above was written, two interesting books have appeared. The first, of 392 pages, is all about the historical Arthur; the second, of over 400 pages, dismisses him in one half-sentence. On Camlan, Professor Higham mentions Castlesteads, but thinks Arthur more likely to have met his fate at the Camlan in mid-Wales, near Mallwyd in the mountain region north-east of Machynlleth.[65] Against that one may say that Castlesteads was a military site, as the Welsh place was not; other evidence overwhelmingly puts Arthur in North Britain, not Wales; and, if Arthur was killed in the Cambrian mountains, it is curious that the Welsh should forget this. As for the second volume, despite frequent reference to Camlan, not a word on where it might have been, for its editors declare that 'a putative historical Arthur is not the concern of this volume'.[66] It is very strange. All the same, it shows the importance of presenting the case for Camlan on the Roman Wall for the events of 536–37.

We can therefore be sure of the following. Arthur really existed; he was a North British warrior with outstanding powers of leadership; his battles seem to have been cattle raids (an ancient Celtic practice) made on British neighbours during the terrible volcanic winter of 536–37; he was not fighting for gold or territory; he was killed on the Roman Wall near Carlisle in 537; he had nothing to do with the British victory of 493 at Mount 'Badon' or Braydon in Wiltshire; but his heroism in saving from starvation the people of Strathclyde (as it seems) made him at first a hero and before long a legend.

Finally, a note on *Camboglanna*. It was the name of the Roman fort at Castlesteads (National Grid Reference NY 5163), above Cam Beck (preserving the name) in Cumbria, and not (as once thought) of Birdoswald (now taken as *Banna*) east of it. Before the 1970s Castlesteads was believed to be *Uxelodunum*, the 'high fort' (which is now placed at Stanwix, by Carlisle). *Camboglanna*, appearing on the Rudge Cup and Amiens *patera*, is recorded in the ninth-century Ravenna Cosmography as *Gabaglanda* and *Cambroianna*. Often explained as 'curved bank' or 'bank at a bend', *Camboglanna* is better taken as 'bank of (the river called) "Cam"', bank of (the) twisting river', since

---

[64] Liebhard 2016, 117, 122.
[65] Higham 2018, 225.
[66] Lloyd-Morgan 2019, 6.

cam is used of many Welsh rivers (Caman, Camen, Cemig, and so on).[67] For all its fame, the site will disappoint modern visitors. The stronghold was flattened in 1791.[68] But many altars survive, one of them to the spirit of Gemellus, *custos armarum*. While he lived, he kept the garrison's weapons fit for use.[69] Even if the fort was small, it had a strategic location, at a spot where Cam Beck joins the Irthing. To its associations with war can be added a new one. There is every reason to think that, in 537, when the walls of this stronghold stood high and it was a tough nut to crack, Arthur was killed by men of Rheged, the British kingdom centred on Penrith. He may have been on a cattle-raid against them; in any case it is likely that his bones lie in an unknown grave somewhere nearby. An anonymous poem in the thirteenth-century Black Book of Carmarthen has the line *Anoeth bid bet y Arthur* (The world's wonder a grave for Arthur), with the implication that nobody knew where Arthur was buried.[70] Obviously, it was not in Wales. Nor is it probable that warriors brought his body back for honourable burial at Govan or elsewhere on the Clyde, because people would have remembered that. It seems that the mortal remains of Arthur (if not thrown by his enemies into the River Cam, as is likely) rest in a roadside field near *Camboglanna* or Camlan or Castlesteads, a fort on Hadrian's Wall.

---

[67] Falileyev 2010, 13, 20.
[68] Clayton 1980, 172.
[69] Ireland 1996, 251.
[70] Jones 2019, 17.

Chapter 3

573: LEGENDS OF MERLIN AT ARFDERYDD OR ARTHURET, CUMBRIA

If locations of other conflicts discussed in this book have been unclear, that of Arfderydd has long been known. In 1868 the Scottish antiquary W. F. Skene (1809–1892) identified it as Arthuret in north-east Cumbria. We can be sure that this battle took place near Carlisle in 573 (or perhaps 575). Nevertheless, more can be said on its location and the meaning of its name. What follows thus has two functions: it reviews what has been written on the conflict between 1860 and 2019, and then sets out a new etymology for *Arfderydd*, with implications for where the action took place.

Annales Cambriae records the encounter under the year 573. The best manu-script here is London, British Library, MS Harley 3859 (copied in about 1100), which has merely *Bellum Armterid*. But London, National Archives, MS E.164/1 (of the thirteenth century) adds to this, saying the encounter was 'between the sons of Eliffer, and Gwenddolau son of Ceidio, in which battle Gwenddolau fell. Merlin went mad.'[1] The mention of Merlin (*Merlinus*, a form deriving from Geoffrey of Monmouth) shows how a historical event has gained the trappings of legend.

A step forward was made by W. F. Skene in his *Four Ancient Books of Wales* (Edinburgh, 1868) and elsewhere, where he identified *Arfderydd* as Arthuret, south of the Esk in what is now Cumbria. Sir John Rhys (1840–1915), fertile in ideas now discredited, describing Carlisle as 'the most important town of the Northern Cumbrians', considered 'much of its importance' lost thanks to the battle, its site identified by some with Arthuret ('and by others with Airdrie', east of Glasgow). The victor was Rhydderch, who 'thereupon fixed his head-quarters on a rock in the Clyde', the massive volcanic height of Dumbarton 'fort of Britons'.[2] If only we could be so sure of events. There seems no

---

[1] Williams ab Ithel 1860, 5.
[2] Rhys 1904, 146.

archaeological evidence for Carlisle as a major centre of population in the sixth century, and it is effectively unknown in early Welsh tradition, unlike the realm of Rheged, with its capital in east Cumbria, at or near Penrith.

Sir John Lloyd, a great historian, agreed with Skene on the site, regarding the encounter as 'a triumph won by Rhydderch [of Strathclyde] over Gwenddoleu ap Ceidio.' Yet he rejected the notion (which Skene thought implied by later hagiography) of its also being a victory of Christianity over semi-paganism.[3] The fame of the battle was discussed by the Chadwicks, whose concern was story rather than history. They referred to the 'Dialogue of Myrddin [= Merlin] and Taliesin', a short but obscure poem in the thirteenth-century Black Book of Carmarthen (= Aberystwyth, National Library of Wales, MS Peniarth 1). It bewails the slaughter of heroes and mentions Maelgwn Gwynedd (d. 547), the sons of Eliffer, and Arfderydd. The Black Book also has Merlin's monologue *Afallenau* (Apple-Trees), where the prophet alludes to Gwenddolau as his generous lord; to Arfderydd, where he wore a torque of gold; and to his present misery as an exile in the woods. Another poem placed in the mouth of Merlin, in the Red Book of Hergest (= Oxford, Jesus College, MS Welsh 1), is called *Cyfoesi* (Conversation). It tells of the great but doomed power of Rhydderch, and mentions the city of the bards by the Clyde, Gwenddolau's death at Arfderydd and Merlin's madness. The Chadwicks also cited the Welsh triads, which mention Gwenddolau's loyal retinue, who 'continued the battle for six weeks after their lord was slain'. The battle likewise figures in a fragment of the 'Herbertian' life of St Kentigern, written in 1147–1164 (when Herbert was bishop of Glasgow). This is known only from London, British Library, MS Titus A xix. The fragment tells of a prophet Lailoken, who went mad while fighting in a battle between Liddel Water and Carwannok after a voice from heaven cursed him for bringing the slaughter about. (Walter Bower's *Scotichronicon*, of the fifteenth century gives a version of this story with the form *Carwanolow.*) Carwannok is usually taken as Carwinley, a farm (National Grid Reference (NGR) NY 4072) in Arthuret parish. Neither toponym appears in the more conventional life of Kentigern written by Jocelyn of Furness in 1175–1199, and surviving in London, British Library, MS Vitellius C viii.[4] Jocelyn's interest in Celtic legends was clearly minimal.

As for the meaning of *Arfderydd*, an advance was made by Sir Ifor Williams, who took the second element as *terydd* (ardent, passionate, fierce).[5] We shall return to this point. Rachel Bromwich spoke of Myrddin or Merlin as a

---

[3] Lloyd 1911, 166–67.
[4] Chadwick and Chadwick 1932, 105–14.
[5] Williams 1935, 161.

Northern hero who was present at Arfderydd, but who was later associated by Geoffrey of Monmouth and others with Carmarthen.[6] Yet few will now agree with her that Myrddin's name is not derived from *Caerfyrddin* (= Carmarthen). Further information on the saga of Arfderydd was given by Jackson. He cited Welsh accounts of the death there of Gwenddolau, son of Ceidio, who was fighting his cousins Gwrgi and Peredur. He quoted the Latin fragment associated with Kentigern for the field of conflict as being on the English side of Liddel Water, near the Roman fort called 'Castra Exploratorum'. He noted how Welsh sources state that Gwrgi and Peredur, deserted by their troops, were killed in 580 at *Caer Greu* (location unknown) by Eda of the Big Knees (identity unknown). Although nothing can be said of the lands which they ruled, Jackson thought that, if Carwinley is called after Gwenddolau, then Arthuret was within his domains.[7]

A brief account of Arfderydd was given by Sir Thomas Parry, who spoke of it as Rhydderch ap Tudwal's victory over Gwenddolau, and of Myrddin's going mad in it, after which this warrior lived in the Wood of Caledonia for 50 years with the wild beasts, mourning Gwenddolau's death. Parry noted that Myrddin must have had a reputation as a prophet by the tenth century, since he figures as such in the Welsh political poem *Armes Prydein* (The Prophecy of Britain) composed in late 940 (after English capitulation to the Vikings at Leicester, the *Lego* and *Arlego* of its text).[8]

The account of the local Roman roads provided long ago by Margary remains valuable, particularly as his conclusions are ignored by some historical maps, which show the road from Carlisle to Birrens and beyond as running directly via the Roman fort of 'Castra Exploratorum' at Netherby. This is incorrect. Margary said as follows. The road ran north from Carlisle along the present A7 Trunk Road. He thought that it then turned west at a point three miles south of Netherby, crossing the Esk at a ford called the Roost, near a farm called the Fauld. Its course west of the river is shown by an *agger* now followed by a footpath (NGR NY 3467) in Millhill Wood, east of Greta. As for the fort at Netherby, this was approached by a subsidiary road which left the main one north of the River Lyne (NGR NY 3965), passed Longtown, and then after Netherby ran northwards through Eskdale along the east bank of the river, where its route is marked by a Roman fort at Broomholm (NGR NY 3781). It eventually reached the fort at Raeburnfoot (NGR NY 2599), there linking up in wild moorland country with another military road running

---

[6] Bromwich 1954.
[7] Jackson 1955.
[8] Parry 1955, 27.

east-west.[9] We shall see how these details are significant for locating Arfderydd. Jackson mentioned Arfderydd in a later study, dating it to 574.[10]

A new phase in our knowledge begins with the work by Jarman. He translated Myrddin's lines of lamentation in *Afalleneu*, which he dated to 850–1050, including the following:

Mirth delights me not, no woman visits me;
And in the battle of Arfderydd my torque was of gold
Though today I am not treasured by one the colour of swans.

Jarman noted further how Myrddin elsewhere in the Black Book of Carmarthen calls Gwenddolau one who was formerly 'a glorious prince / Gathering booty from every border'; but how 'beneath the brown earth, now he is silent'. Meanwhile, Rhydderch knows little of Myrddin's misery, with 'Snow up to my hips among the forest wolves, / Icicles in my hair'. The contrast of Gwenddolau, a shadowy figure, and Rhydderch, the sixth-century ruler of Strathclyde, known from Adamnán's life of Columba, *Historia Brittonum* and Jocelyn's life of Kentigern is evident. Jarman at this time believed that Rhydderch was the victor at Arfderydd, though no early source states this.[11] If so, saga would shed a little light on history.

Jarman made other important comments on Arfderydd in his Cardiff inaugural lecture. He described Myrddin as purely legendary. There is no reason to take him as a contemporary of the North British bards Aneirin and Taliesin; his name derives from *Caerfyrddin* (= Carmarthen), misunderstood as 'Myrddin's stronghold', though the correct meaning is 'stronghold of the sea-fortress', with no allusion to any person. Jarman here disagreed with Rachel Bromwich. He again said that Welsh saga points to Arfderydd as a victory for Rhydderch.[12] The Caledonian Forest where Merlin froze in misery was identified by Count Tolstoy. He quoted Hector Boece, who (as translated by Bellenden) said, 'The watter of Clyde [...] risis out of the samin montane within the wood of Calidone, fra quhilk risis Annand.'[13] So it was the area around Beattock Summit (NGR NS 9915), where modern road and railway cross the 1,000-foot contour. The region is bleak in winter even now, as proved by graves of nineteenth-century travellers who perished in the snow. Hence the legend of Merlin, Scotland's man of the mountain.

---

[9] Margary 1955–57, II, 186, 191.
[10] Jackson 1958.
[11] Jarman 1959.
[12] Jarman 1960, 17–23.
[13] Tolstoy 1961–3.

The genealogies of Gwenddolau and his supposed antagonist Rhydderch were conveniently set out by Bartrum.[14] Arfderydd is marked, west of the Esk, on the Ordnance Survey (OS) Map for the period.[15] In his revised edition of a Black Book poem, Jarman made no fundamental changes to his views of Arfderydd.[16] Jackson noted how tales of Arfderydd are among much other material to enter Welsh tradition from the Old North.[17] Alcock (following Skene) gave the battle's name as 'Arderydd', even though Lloyd showed 60 years previously that this is incorrect.[18] In her edition of Sir Ifor Williams's papers, Rachel Bromwich noted Skene's identification of *Arfderydd* as Arthuret, and H. M. Chadwick's suggestion that Gwenddoleu's stronghold was the nearby Roman fortress of 'Castra Exploratorum' or Netherby. While Williams at one point dated Arfderydd to 573, he elsewhere gave 575, following Lloyd and the Chadwicks. This later dating has not had the attention it deserves, but it may be right.[19]

Clarke's edition of Geoffrey of Monmouth's life of Merlin has a long note on Arfderydd. The editor explained that a tradition in the Welsh triads, on how it was fought for a lark's nest, may not be trivial, for it perhaps refers to Caerlaverock (lark fort) at the mouth of the Nith. (Even if this appears dubious, Jackson still came to regard the location as possible.) He discounted Skene's identification of the fort of Carwannok as being Liddel Strength (NGR NY 4074), because this defence is too late, being a motte-and-bailey with added keep. The Roman fort of 'Castra Exploratum' at Netherby seemed more likely. Clarke described the battlefield as unlocated, but ruled out the shallow earthwork of the Knowes of Arthuret as of the thirteenth century. He preferred a site on high ground near Arthuret's isolated parish church, south of Longtown. Yet a site by the fords of Esk, which may have shifted in 14 centuries, is also possible.[20] Although the present paper closes by arguing for a site four miles north-north-east of Arthuret church, Clarke's account is still useful for discussing questions neglected by others.

On the subject of the forces involved, Morris was categorical. 'It was a battle between different branches of the Coel dynasty (usually located in Kyle, Ayrshire). The kings of York combined with Dunaut of the Pennines to destroy their cousin Gwendoleu, who ruled in the Carlisle region.'[21] In contrast to

---

[14] Bartrum 1966, 73, 89.
[15] *Map of Britain in the Dark Ages.*
[16] Jarman 1967, 11–17.
[17] Jackson 1969, 63.
[18] Alcock 1971, 83.
[19] Williams 1972, 86, 123.
[20] Clarke 1973, 160–62.
[21] Morris 1973, 218.

this misplaced assurance is one respected history of Scotland, which mentions Rhydderch of Strathclyde as attacking Bernicia in 579–586. but makes no reference to Arfderydd.[22] Molly Miller attempted to recreate the political situation leading up to the struggle.[23] Jackson moved from earlier early scepticism on the question of the 'lark's nest' as *casus belli* to regarding it as the name of a nearby fort.[24]

Rachel Bromwich said much on Arfderydd. It was a conflict between British factions. The English had no part in it. The surviving allusions unfortunately leave unclear why and by whom it was fought. If, as the triads and other late evidence state, Gwenddolau was there killed by Gwrgi and Peredur, then it was between first cousins, as the genealogies reveal. No early testimony shows that Rhydderch of Strathclyde was there, despite Skene's assertions, followed by Lloyd. She also set out statements by Robert Vaughan (d. 1667), antiquary and collector of manuscripts, on the struggle as due to a 'lark's nest', which she thought might reflect early tradition.[25] Jarman pointed out how Lloyd considered '573' as an error for '575'. He stressed that this part of *Annales Cambriae* is considered reliable and most scholars agree that the forces met at Arthuret. After that come difficulties. We cannot be sure that Rhydderch was there. Jarman thought plausible the arguments of Molly Miller, that Rhydderch was not concerned in it, that the struggle was a family feud among descendants of Coel (and so not involving Rhydderch) and that Gwrgi and Peredur came from the Lancashire/Yorkshire region and were allies with Dunawd of Cumbria, while from Strathclyde came Cynfelyn Drwsgl. During a lull in the fighting, Dinogad, son of Cynan Garwyn, made his escape, to his eternal shame. But Jarman admitted that almost all the tradition is legendary in character and hardly a basis for firm historical conclusions.[26] Jenny Rowland underlines the partisan elements in the recorded traditions, with strong sympathy for Gwenddolau (the defeated hero) and lack of it for the victors.[27] Clare Stancliffe, citing David Dumville, describes the annals of 573 onwards as 'drawn from entries of contemporary events written into the margins of Easter tables, apparently in north Britain'.[28] Richard Coates explains *Arfderydd*, after a suggestion of Sir Ifor Williams in the English Place-Name Society volume for Cumberland, as perhaps 'strong place, swift place'.[29] Despite the statements

---

[22] Duncan 1975, 60.

[23] Miller 1975, 96–118.

[24] Jackson 1977, 45–50.

[25] Bromwich 1978, 208–10, 540.

[26] Jarman 1978.

[27] Rowland 1990, 98, 112.

[28] Stancliffe 1995, 84–96.

[29] Coates and Breeze 2000, 281.

of Jarman and Stancliffe, Oliver Padel regards some early entries in *Annales Cambriae* as 'legendary', including that on the deaths of Gwrgi and Peredur (the victors of Arfderydd) in 580.[30] David Dumville's distrust is more drastic. He excludes them completely from his edition, though he has useful notes on the Public Record Office text as perhaps copied at Neath, Glamorgan.[31] Nick Higham is also wary, taking the sixth-century entries for North Britain as mere reconstructions by a Strathclyde cleric in the late eighth century.[32]

In his final paper on Merlin, Jarman criticized Molly Miller for neglecting traditions on Lailoken in Latin texts from Scotland. But he took seriously Jackson's contention that the 'lark's nest' of tradition comes from a very real struggle for the stronghold of Caerlaverock.[33] In a wide-ranging survey, Catherine Daniel states that Merlin went mad 'pendant la bataille d'Arfderyd [*sic*] avant de se retirer dans la forêt de Célidon'.[34] Koch's new atlas accepts Margary in its plotting of Roman roads, but follows the OS in placing the battlefield west of the Esk, towards Millhill Wood.[35] The New Edinburgh History of Scotland then had a passage on the battle which is brief enough to quote entire.

The tenth-century Cambro-Latin chronicle *Annales Cambriae* consists for this period of excerpts from a lost eighth-century chronicle from the North British zone. It records a battle at *Armterid* in 573, probably Arthuret on the river Esk, some seven kilometres north (*recte*, five kilometres north-north-east) of Longtown in Liddesdale. Medieval Welsh literature claimed a great deal about this battle, associating it with fictional and historical characters (including Aedán and Merlin), but it provides little useful evidence. The brothers who apparently won the battle of Arthuret were cousins of Urbgen's father Cinmarch, their deaths recorded in 580. It may, therefore, be that Urbgen (= Urien in Welsh tradition) succeeded one or both of them as king (of Rheged), and flourished into the 590s, as *Historia Brittonum* envisions.[36]

An even fuller account of Arthuret, including details of Skene's fieldwork there and his attempts to locate the conflict, deserves careful attention, all the more so because it was cited but not discussed in the original published version of this chapter.[37] Its account of local archaeological remains can be compared with the conclusions below, arrived at on a different basis, from

---

[30] Padel 2000, 12.
[31] Dumville 2002, viii.
[32] Higham 2002, 198–89.
[33] Jarman 2003.
[34] Daniel 2006, 7.
[35] Koch 2007, map 21.3.
[36] Fraser 2009, 12.
[37] Clarkson 2010, 88–99.

analysis of river names. In the same year the conflict figured in two other books. In the first, it appears briefly in the context of Geoffrey of Monmouth's fictions.[38] In the second, it is related to the difficult and obscure subject of early Welsh prophecy.[39] Both take us some way away from the real events which are the theme of this book, and particularly of this chapter, its arguments first appearing soon after.[40]

Since then, Arfderydd has figured (with one sentence) in a book covering similar ground, but written in a way unlike that of the present one.[41] The arguments put forward in 2012 on the battle's location are now taken up in a full-scale account of Merlin traditions.[42] There is also an account of it by a German independent scholar, whose reproducing (at some expense) of modern maps for this and other Dark Age battlefields deserves praise.[43] Arthuret is treated as well by a US scholar, whose chapter is one of the best in a collection flawed by a decision to ignore much scholarship published since 1997.[44]

And so we come to the final part, indicating how linguistic analysis aids us in a quest for battlefields and the meaning of the names. Citing Sir Ifor Williams, Richard Coates has proposed a sense 'swift place'. This needs revision. Another approach appears more cogent. There are three points to make. First, in Celtic river names, allusions to heat or fire are common. The Teinntidh near Callander is the 'fiery one' (cf. Gaelic *teine* 'fire'), from its 'rapid boiling course'; the Evelix (with English plural) near Dornoch is the 'ember' (Gaelic *eibhleag*); Aberlosk, in the hills east of Moffat, is the confluence of the 'burning stream' (cf. Welsh *llosgi* 'to burn').[45] Second, other Celtic hydronyms allude to tools or weapons. Abergele in North Wales is 'mouth of (the stream called) blade'; Aberdaugleddyf (= Milford Haven) is 'mouth of two (rivers called) "swords"'; a tributary of the Eastern Cleddau 'sword', near Haverfordwest, is the Cyllell 'knife' (= Cartlett Brook); the Rhymni near Cardiff is 'borer, auger'; and so on.[46] Third is the translation 'strong, swift' for *terydd*. This is a dubious guess of lexicographers. The original sense is 'ardent, passionate, fierce' (as pointed out by Ifor Williams in 1935), according with possible derivation of *terydd* from Latin *torridus* 'burning, fiery, scorching'.[47] That helps as regards

---

[38] Jankulak 2010, 89, 91.
[39] Williams 2010, 93–4, 103.
[40] Breeze 2012a.
[41] Halsall 2013, 23.
[42] Clarkson 2016, 59–60.
[43] Liebhard 2016, 66–69.
[44] Bollard 2019, 36, 43.
[45] Watson 1926, 443, 460.
[46] Thomas 1938, 100.
[47] *Geiriadur* 1950–2002, 3487.

Arfderydd. A first element here meaning 'place', as Ifor Williams proposed, is doubtful. In contrast are Welsh *arf* and Cornish *arv*, meaning 'weapon' and derived from Latin *arma* (arms). Welsh *terydd* is translated as 'ardent, fierce; flaming, blazing'. This allows translation of *Armterid* or *Arfderydd* as 'ardent weapon, burning weapon', and suggests strongly that it was, in origin, the name of a stream or river. There would be nothing surprising in this. Many rivers, red with the blood of combatants, have given their names to battles: the *Uinued* or Went in 655; Bannockburn, 1314; Boyne, 1690; Marne, 1914; Somme, 1916; Ebro, 1938; Imjin, 1951; and so on.

What does this imply for the site of battle? It must be taken with the statement in the fragmentary life of Kentigern, repeated by Walter Bower (d. 1449), that the forces met in an open space between Liddel Water and Carwannok or Carwanolow, normally regarded as Carwinley (NGR NY 4072). This would accord with the arguments cited above. Margary pointed to the existence of a route north from Netherby that led up the east side of Eskdale. Troops taking it southwards would naturally pass Carwinley; to get there they may have crossed the ford (NGR NY 4175) on Liddel Water two miles north of it. As for Arfderydd, this may be interpreted as the old name of Carwinley Burn, which runs westwards through a wooded dell to enter the Esk, and still forms the northern boundary of the parish of Arthuret. It may also explain a peculiarity of Arthuret as a parish with no ancient village or centre. If its name was initially a hydronym, applying to no settlement, that will make sense. Arthuret would thus resemble Brent or Thame in England (but not Hull in Yorkshire, from the English settlement-name *Hula* (huts), as at Hoole in north Lancashire), or Tain, Nairn, Banff, Leith, Irvine, Ayr and Annan in Scotland, or Douglas in the Isle of Man, as a place named after a river.

This argument seems cogent. It brings together what we can gather of early lines of communication, place names and the statements of medieval Scottish writers. If it is objected that Carwinley Burn already has a British name, being called after Gwenddolau who fell in the combat, we may reply that it must have been called something before him. Perhaps it gained its new name because he fought on its banks during that tragic day, possibly at Carwinley itself. The first element *Car-* need indicate no city or other stronghold. Jackson observed long ago that in Cumbric this element often meant 'simply a hamlet or manor-house and farm, originally protected by some kind of defensive stockade' or the like.[48] So the isolated farm of Carwinley may, apparently, pay its own tribute to that battle long ago.

---

[48] Jackson 1963, 60–84.

If this reasoning on the meaning of *Arfderydd* is correct, we can locate precisely an early battlefield of North Britain. It lay on the road from Eskdale to Netherby, south of Liddel Water and close to Carwinley Burn. This was at the time known as *Arfderydd* (burning weapon), a form resembling other Celtic hydronyms, where rivers are compared to fire or are called 'spear', 'blade', 'lance', 'sword' and even 'needle' because 'their waters flash brightly'.[49] To this day Arthuret's parish boundary runs along this stream. How far that casts light on the political and military events leading up to the encounter may be left to others. Yet we may point out that it should interest archaeologists as well as historians. Since the battle was considered decisive and was fought on a large scale, archaeologists may discover traces of sixth-century armour, weapons or the like in its vicinity. If they do they will bring us closer to the events of that day, neither the first nor the last of battles between North British kinsmen, but having permanent and international effects in bringing the legend of Merlin to birth.

---

[49] Owen and Morgan 2007, 7, 456.

Chapter 4

C. 590: PICTS AT GWEN YSTRAD OR THE RIVER WINSTER, CUMBRIA

Among the problems of early Northern history is the location of Gwen Ystrad, where sixth-century Britons commanded by Urien of Rheged repelled an attack. The assault, apparently made by Pictish sea raiders, is described vividly in a poem of Taliesin. But Gwen Ystrad has been unidentified, although it was clearly in Rheged, a territory with its heartland around Penrith, and extending into Lancashire, south-west Scotland and north Yorkshire. In what follows there is a review of previous discussion and then a solution, in which the manuscript's 'Gwen Ystrad' is emended to *Gwensteri* or the River Winster, Cumbria. Despite the novelty of the emendation, we shall see that a location on the Winster was proposed as far back as the 1850s. Admirers of the Victorians will be encouraged to find nineteenth-century scholarship seemingly vindicated in the twenty-first.

Modern awareness of the conflict began in the eighteenth century, when the earliest Welsh poetry (of about the year 600) started to appear in print. In a pioneer collection of Welsh verse and prose, Taliesin's poem on Gwen Ystrad was presented with a translation, declaring that raiders 'came in a body to Gwenystrad to offer battle; neither the fields nor the woods afforded protection to their enemies when they came in their fury, like the roaring wave rushing in its might to cover the beach'. It was accompanied by another rousing battle poem of Taliesin, on Argoed Llwyfain (possibly by the River Lyvennet, south of Penrith), where Urien Rheged vanquished the English leader Fflamddwyn, leaving 'many a dead carcase', so that 'ravens were coloured' as they picked at English corpses. The editors of the poems described Urien as 'King of Cumbria'. But more pertinent is a third poem attributed to Taliesin, which praises not Urien of Rheged but Gwallawg, who ruled the former British kingdom of Elmet, east of Leeds. It recounts his victories, including one on the Gwensteri, long identified as the River Winster, south-east of Windermere.[1]

---

[1] Jones, Williams, and Pughe 1870, 47–49, 55–56.

These poems in the fourteenth-century Book of Taliesin reappear in an edition famed for the accuracy of its text and the absurdity of its commentary. The absurdity appears in its explanation of 'Gwen Ystrad' as 'warrior's dale', its locating near Carmarthen and its identification of Gwensteri as Basingwerk, Flintshire.[2] No surprise that Sir John Lloyd (1861–1947) alluded to the obscurity of 'these warlike strains, in which the setting is Cumbrian rather than Welsh'.[3] Hugh Williams (1843–1911), taking our three poems as genuinely archaic, similarly spoke of the beauty of verses 'amid a host of lines extremely difficult to understand'.[4] Progress came in 1918, with an epoch-making edition of Taliesin by Sir John Morris-Jones (1864–1929), distinguishing some dozen authentic poems of the sixth century from spurious later ones. It was cited, with W. F. Skene's *Four Ancient Books of Wales* of 1868, by W. J. Watson (1865–1948) of Edinburgh, who quoted lines on 'blood-stained men laying down their arms' at Gwen Ystrad, while 'leaders named their hostages' as 'waves washed the tails of their horses'. Watson, translating 'Gwen Ystrad' as 'white strath' or even 'holy strath', remarked that Skene took it as the Gala valley of Galashiels in south-east Scotland, but Morris-Jones as Wensleydale, Yorkshire. Yet he noted how the poem speaks of combat by the sea, which rules these out. He reasoned that, since the enemies were 'men of Prydyn' and so not Britons but Picts (notorious for piracy until the ninth century, when their power collapsed), 'what Taliesin describes has all the appearance of a Pictish raid on the Solway coast of Rheged', Urien's domain.[5] His observation has been strangely neglected.

It is ignored by Lloyd-Jones, who referred merely to Morris-Jones on 'Gwen Ystrad' as Wensleydale. As for *Gwensteri*, Lloyd-Jones criticized Skene's taking it as the Winster in Cumbria, on the grounds that, if it were a river name, it should have *ar* (on) before it and not *yg* (in). He also thought unlikely the earlier suggestion of Thomas Stephens that it denoted 'Gwen Ystrad'.[6] It did not occur to him what will be argued here: *Gwensteri* resembles a known place name, that of the Winster, whereas nobody has ever identified 'Gwen Ystrad'; and it is more likely for *Gwensteri* to be corrupted (in a manuscript notorious for corruption) to the easier 'Gwen Ystrad' (white valley) than the reverse. *Gwensteri* is the *lectio difficilior*, 'Gwen Ystrad' a *lectio facilior*. The implications of this are set out below.

---

[2] Evans 1910, 29–30, 56–57, 60, 108–109, 156.
[3] Lloyd 1911, 170.
[4] Williams 1912, 430.
[5] Watson 1926, 344–45.
[6] Lloyd-Jones 1931–63, 663.

The three poems were analysed briefly by the Chadwicks. That mentioning Gwensteri is their number XI, those on Gwen Ystrad and Argoed Llwyfain are, respectively, XXXI and XXXV.[7] Urien Rheged's struggles against Theodric (572–79) and Hussa (585–92) of Bernicia figure in a summary history.[8] A brilliant account of Taliesin, with a translation of the poem on Argoed Llwyfain, was given by Sir Ifor Williams (1881-1965).[9] Urien's besieging of Theodric, son of Ida, at Lindisfarne in about 575 (according to *Historia Brittonum*) was mentioned by Kenneth Jackson (1909–1991).[10]

An important account of the early poetry was provided by Rachel Bromwich. She quoted Morris-Jones on Wensleydale as perhaps the site of Gwen Ystrad, again without mention of Watson and the Solway region. She described Taliesin as claiming to have witnessed this 'defensive battle turned to overwhelming victory', translating his lines on how, at 'the approach to the ford I saw bloodstained men lay down their arms in front of the grey weirs'.[11] The career of Urien Rheged and the extent of his realm ('it seems probable that its heartland was the Solway plains around Carlisle and Annan') were summed up by Kenneth Jackson, who added that poems to him and to his son Owein 'do not tell us much about them', especially on their battles, 'of which some if not all were against the English'.[12] Watson's belief that Gwen Ystrad was a defeat of Picts, not English, is once more passed over. The poem's simile 'Like waves loud-roaring over the earth / I saw stout men in hosts' was admired by Sir Thomas Parry.[13] A clue to the origins of those doughty Pictish warriors was given in a study of them. The Picts 'possessed a fleet of considerable strength, which implies navigational skill, familiarity with difficult waters, and a knowledge of shipbuilding', so that Pictish naval power is mentioned in the Irish annals.[14] Urien was discussed again by Kenneth Jackson as regards the form *Ulien* in a Latin life of St Kentigern, on which he gave a phonological explanation, never thinking that it is merely a scribal error.[15] This encourages us to emend texts which make no sense. An essay by Sir Idris Foster on Welsh tradition helps little, for it hardly concerns North Britain.[16] Yet a map for the period, although not recording these battles in Taliesin's poetry, is useful in

---

[7] Chadwick and Chadwick 1932, 39.
[8] Williams 1941, 77.
[9] Williams 1944, 63–65.
[10] Jackson 1953, 213.
[11] Bromwich 1954.
[12] Jackson 1955.
[13] Parry 1955, 4.
[14] Wainwright 1955.
[15] Jackson 1958.
[16] Foster 1965.

showing Roman roads vital for post-Roman armies (there was none along the coast of south Cumbria, with tidal inlets that to this day impede communication by land).[17] At this date a brave attempt to relate place names in these poems to those in *Historia Brittonum* was made by D. P. Kirby.[18]

Fifty years after Morris-Jones edited the poetry of Taliesin, a new edition in English allowed further advances. Stephens in 1852 is therein cited for Gwen Ystrad as Winsterdale, Skene in 1868 for it as the valley of Gala Water, and Morris-Jones himself in 1918 for Wensleydale (on the basis of a dubious form in Camden's *Britannia* of 1586). But, yet again, no word on Watson's supposed Pictish raid on the Cumbrian coast, with the editor actually rejecting Morris-Jones's emendation of manuscript *Prydein* (Britain) to *Prydyn* (Picts, Pictland). A *lectio facilior* is preferred to a *lectio difficilior*. However, *Gwensteri* in the poem to Gwallawg of Elmet is taken to refer to the Winster, which until the local government reforms of 1974 separated Westmorland from Lancashire-Beyond-the-Sands.[19] The Gwallawg who fought on the Winster was later described as a Northern hero present at the siege of Lindisfarne in about 575, although with the claim that he was not the ruler of Elmet on the lower Aire.[20] The last view seems dubious. They were surely the same person.

At this time came an updated translation of the poem on Gwen Ystrad, here given complete.

Catraeth's men are up at daybreak
For a conquering prince, cattle-raider.
Urien is he, far-famed chieftain,
He bridles monarchs and hews them,
Strong in war, true lord of Christians,
Pictland's men, deadly war-bands.
Gwen Ystrad your post, battle-honer:
Neither field nor forest was spared,
Land's bulwark, by the force that came.
Like waves roaring harsh onto shore
I saw savage men in war-bands:
And after morning's fray, torn flesh.
I saw border-crossing forces dead,
Strong and angry the clamour one heard.
Defending Gwen Ystrad one saw

---

[17] *Map of Britain.*
[18] Kirby 1967, 23–24.
[19] Williams 1968, 31, 126.
[20] Jackson 1969, 24.

A thin rampart and lone weary men.
At the ford I saw men stained with blood
Downing arms before a grey-haired lord:
They wished peace, for they found the way barred,
Hands crossed, on the strand, cheeks pallid.
Their lords wondered at Idon's rich wine;
Waves washed the tails of their horses.
I saw pillaging men blunted
And blood spattering their garments,
And quick close-grouping for battle:
Battle's cloak, not of flight was his thought,
Rheged's lord, I marvel, when challenged.
I saw noble men about Urien
When he cut down his foes in Llech Wen.
Routing foes in wrath gave him joy,
Men's bucklers were borne where needed:
Lust for battle never leaves Urien.
> And until I die, old,
> By death's strict demand,
> I shall not be joyful
> Unless I praise Urien.[21]

Clancy, like Watson but unlike Ifor Williams, saw the raiders as Picts and not
Britons. 'Catraeth' is usually taken as Catterick, Yorkshire. 'Idon' is (doubt-
fully) understood as the River Eden. 'Llech Wen' ('white rock') has previously
been unidentified, though it is below taken as Whitbarrow, a rocky hill three
miles long and looking down on the Winster.

Whatever the location of Gwen Ystrad, it involved a river. Leslie Alcock
hence commented on the strategic importance of fords at this date (bridges
in highland Britain being few, especially once the Roman army left), so that
Taliesin's fellow-bard Aneirin praised a Gododdin warrior who was 'steady in
guarding the ford'. Seven of Arthur's twelve battles in *Historia Brittonum* were
fought on rivers. (They can now be identified. Six of them were in southern
Scotland: four on the Douglas near Lanark; one on Mouse Water near Carstairs,
or else on the Tarras near Langholm; and one at Dreva on the Upper Tweed.
There was a seventh conflict on the River Glen, Northumberland.) Their
compiler regarded river crossings as obvious places for conflict. It has been
claimed that a handful of British cavalrymen could there rout Anglo-Saxon

---

[21] Clancy 1970, 24–25.

infantry. An emphasis on conflict by rivers in any case shows how 'warfare was open and mobile, and that strongholds or prepared positions played no great part in it'.[22] Alcock's remarks indicate the data to be gained even from heroic verse strong on eulogy but short on facts. Chronicles and poems on the North Britons were referred to by Sir Frank Stenton.[23] In his collected papers, Sir Ifor Williams gave reasons for regarding the Gwallawg of the poems as the ruler of Elmet in the late sixth century. He said further, on editing a ninth-century praise-poem on the fortress at Tenby, Pembrokeshire, that its line, 'They will leave the grey-green ocean to the tribe of Picts', shows them as the terror of the seas before Vikings became a still greater one.[24]

Further evidence for the early reputation of the Picts comes from three post-Roman sources. St Patrick in the fifth century referred to 'most worthless, evil, and apostate Picts', who had bought Christian slaves, Patrick's own Irish converts, from 'soldiers of Coroticus', ruler of Strathclyde. The fifth-century life of St Germanus states that Picts in the year 429 joined forces with the Saxons in a battle against the Britons. Presumably ships were involved. On this, Gildas in the summer of 536 is explicit. He describes repeated Pictish raids in the years immediately after the Roman withdrawal, with the attacks made from the sea, like those of the Scots from Ireland.[25] On Taliesin and Urien, John Morris said much, yet nothing on Gwen Ystrad.[26] Archibald Duncan mentions Aneirin and Urien Rheged, but not Taliesin.[27] Hunter Blair had similar brief remarks on 'the vigorous splendour of this battle poetry'.[28] The introduction to a volume on early Welsh poetry has no bearing on the question except in a remark on Morris-Jones's 'profuse and, as many would believe, arbitrary emendations' in his 1918 edition of Taliesin.[29] It has a bearing on Gwen Ystrad. Conservative critics refuse both to emend this form here or (for reasons of rhyme) to accept Morris-Jones's revision of manuscript *Prydein* (Britain) to *Prydyn* (Picts, Pictland), although both introduce meaning to lines which make no sense as they stand. A fundamental account of Urien Rheged, describing his kingdom as including 'Carlisle, Annan, and the Eden valley' is again silent on Gwen Ystrad.[30]

Work on Taliesin nevertheless allowed Professor Sawyer of Leeds, citing the doubts of David Dumville on the authenticity even of the oldest poems attributed

---

[22] Alcock 1971, 344–45.
[23] Stenton 1971, 76–77.
[24] Williams 1972, 82, 161.
[25] Anderson 1973, 128.
[26] Morris 1973, 232–37.
[27] Duncan 1975, 59–61.
[28] Hunter Blair 1976, 34–35.
[29] Bromwich 1978a, 516–20.
[30] Bromwich 1978b, 516–20.

to the bard, to comment on them as 'evidence for the attitudes and ideals of the sixth century, not for the details about either events or individuals'.[31] Against that we may say that, if careful study can recover information on people, places, and things, his remark will be less true. The famous passage in *Historia Brittonum* on Taliesin and Aneirin as 'illustrious' in poetry during the age of Urien is now easily found.[32] Linguistic and other objections to the poetry attributed to them were made by Wendy Davies, who feels that they lack the authority of normal historical documents.[33] There is truth in this. Yet poetry can still tell the historian things which charters or chronicles cannot. Instances are provided by Patrick Sims-Williams, who sees parallels between the verse of Taliesin and sixth-century Latin panegyric. In the sixth century, for example, Corippus praised the Emperor Justin for holding 'firm reins on kings who must be ruled', while Taliesin described Urien as one who 'curbs princes and cuts them down'.[34] Apart from sycophancy, which eternally shadows the great, there is an implication of a British debt to Latin rhetoric. Yet David Dumville questions whether Urien's power was as great as the poems imply. Taliesin calls him 'ruler of Catterick', even when by the late sixth century this Yorkshire place was in English hands. He concludes either that the Catraeth of the poems has been misidentified, or that the poems are later forgeries.[35] A third possibility, that Urien claimed territory where his writ no longer ran (like ex-kings or governments in exile of all ages), is not considered. Court poets and propagandists being professionally blind to political realities and the degrading realm of fact, we need not believe that Taliesin was on oath when acting as wordsmith-for-hire.

Here we come to crucial evidence. One of Taliesin's two poems to Gwallawg praises him as defender of 'delightful Llan Llennawg', which has been identified with 'Staynlenok', an unidentified place near Millom in southwest Cumbria.[36] If so, it tends to confirm 'Gwensteri' in the same poem as the Winster or Winsterdale. Taliesin's paeans to Urien as demonstrating knowledge of Latin poetry, as well as Northern geography, are alluded to elsewhere.[37] In a full-length analysis of the poem on Gwen Ystrad, Graham Isaac dismisses a sixth-century date for the poem and allocates it to the later eleventh century.[38] The present paper will, of course, fail in its purpose if it does

---

[31] Sawyer 1978, 18.
[32] Whitelock 1979, 262.
[33] Davies 1982, 210.
[34] Sims-Williams 1984.
[35] Dumville 1988.
[36] Rowland 1990, 101n.102.
[37] Davies 1995, 5, 20.
[38] Isaac 1998.

not turn Dr Isaac's arguments upside down and restore the poem to the earlier date. Gwallawg figures in an anonymous eulogy of Cadwallon of Gwynedd, who ravaged Northumbria in 633–34. It states that 'Brave Gwallawg prepared / Destruction of Catraeth [Catterick], great and renowned'.[39] Despite their obscurity, the lines show Gwallawg as a Northerner and a force to be reckoned with. Nick Higham supplies useful references to Rheged's 'much-vaunted literary association with King Urien, Taliesin's putative patron', including Sims-Williams's arguments 'against Urien as a recoverable figure of history', which Professor Higham imagines are strong.[40]

As for Taliesin's praise-poem and elegy to Gwallawg, these were translated and commented on in 2002. They are impressive poetry. The first refers to his defence of 'pleasant Llan Lleennog' or Llennawg, placed near Millom. It refers as well to combats near Edinburgh and Bathgate, 'provocation for York', 'a battle on the Winster, subduing the English' and the like. As for the elegy, this claims of Gwallawg that 'Wealthy men in torques pledge themselves / From Dumbarton to Caradoc' (that is, from the Clyde to the Wye between Hereford and Ross, where the settlement of Caradoc stands to this day).[41] Although subsequent research corrects identification of other toponyms in the first poem, what matters here is its allusion to Winsterdale as place of combat, here not with Picts but the English.

On reference in a ninth-century poem on Tenby to stormy weather as when only Picts would be at sea, Geraint Gruffydd observes that by this date the real danger came from Vikings, not Picts. He regards 'Picts' as used for any sea raiders, no matter what language they spoke.[42] It still demonstrates the evil reputation of Pictish pirates. Nick Higham confuses what I said on Taliesin's poems to Urien (which are datable to the sixth century) with anonymous poems on Urien (of the eighth or ninth).[43] John Koch plots several of our toponyms. He rightly puts Urien's kingdom of Rheged in Cumbria but misplaces Urien's 'Yrechwydd'. It was instead in north Yorkshire, bordering the *Echwydd* or 'fresh water', the marshes of the Ouse, once a major obstacle to communication below York.[44] This casts light on Urien's power. Anglo-Saxon threats notwithstanding, Urien claimed authority in Yrechwydd, linked with Rheged by the Roman road over Stainmore. Like the kings of medieval

---

[39] Breeze 2001.
[40] Higham 2001.
[41] Breeze 2002b.
[42] Gruffydd 2002, 24.
[43] Higham 2002, 177.
[44] Koch 2007, map 21.3.

Navarre, whose realm straddled the Pyrenees (but has long been partioned by France and Spain), Urien ruled both sides of an upland barrier.

An excursus on Taliesin and Urien Rheged by a historian (not a linguist) records dispute between those who argue that 'a sixth-century horizon cannot be proven', the poems being the work of a later age, and those who believe that 'painstaking analysis does prove that the poetry was first composed in the sixth century'.[45] The latter view is maintained here. The better we understand the geographical background of these poems, the weaker the case for regarding them as later forgeries. Geography recurs as regards reports by Gildas of Pictish attacks by sea, where his reference to 'overseas' puzzles one commentator.[46] Yet Scotland has many islands off its coast. Before the Irish settled in Argyll and beyond in the fifth century, they would have been inhabited by Picts, so that Gildas's 'overseas' need not be problematic. In any case, nobody doubts that the Picts 'launched their seaborne attacks' from the north. Anyone on the coast might fear to wake up one morning and find these raiders at the door.

Tim Clarkson of Manchester discusses the poem on Gwen Ystrad, rightly agreeing with Graham Isaac in rejecting Ifor Williams's emended *rywin idon* (plentiful wine of Idon or River Eden) (the Eden, in north Cumbria, is not famous for vineyards). But we need not follow him in taking seriously Isaac's dismissal of Rheged as in Cumbria, or sixth-century origins for the text.[47] For one thing, to cite Watson's observation of 1926 yet again, the poem describes an attack from the sea. Cumbria having a coast, it was open to such attack. For another, the attackers were Picts; and no Welsh poet of the eleventh century cared about them. So the notion that these lines are a late forgery will not detain us. Their place names and politics, to say nothing of the obscurity of their language, accord with a sixth-century dating.

We may therefore be sceptical as regards scepticism in an important paper on north-western topography, where the author considers the 'historicity of Rheged and a great king named Urien is uncertain, if not thoroughly dubious'.[48] We may likewise doubt the view that 'the argument for the authenticity of Taliesin poems' (such as the one on Argoed Llwyfain) 'which appeals to their apparent "realism" has lost much of its force following Ifor Williams's demonstration that many of the poems attributed to Taliesin were in fact intended to be spoken by the bard in ninth-century or later sagas about him'.[49] A bard in Wales might well create a dramatic scene. But he would have

---

[45] Fraser 2009, 125.
[46] George 2009, 49–50.
[47] Clarkson 2010, 72–73.
[48] McCarthy 2011.
[49] Sims-Williams 2011, 91.

little interest in, or knowledge of, sixth-century Northern geography or politics. Professor Sims-Williams confuses the 'realism' of a dramatic encounter (which any skilled poet might invent) with the 'realism' of references to events, place, status or details of weapons or armour (virtually impossible for later writers to invent, even if they wanted to). As for archaeologists who position Rheged as around Stranraer, north of the Solway Firth, or in Lakeland, the evidence tends to the last, for the poems indicate, in the opinion of Phythian-Adams, 'a strategic location guarding the Stainmore pass and the approach road from Deira into Cumbria'.[50] Chronicle, genealogy, a saint's life (that of Kentigern of Glasgow) and verse together offer the image of Urien as a great king and warlord, whose domain extended as far north as the Aeron or River Ayr (for Aeron is not Yorkshire's Aire, with a Norse name) and as far east as Yrechwydd or Yorkshire north of the Ouse marshes.[51]

In the debate on the poetry of Taliesin and Aneirin, we hence align ourselves with the 'cheerfully constructive' tendency represented by John Koch of Aberystwyth, and not the scepticism of Oliver Padel and Graham Isaac.[52] The more we remove the obscurities in Taliesin's poems, the more authentic they appear to be. We may recall this on reading that a 'battle at Catraeth is probably neither that of Degsastan nor that of Gwen Ystrad', where Professor T. O. Clancy is more correct than he knows.[53] 'Degsastan' or, better, *Deguistan* (Dewi's stone) in 603, a Bernician defeat of Scots and Irish, will have been west of Dawyck (Dewi's farm) House on the Upper Tweed. (The stone, five foot high, stands by the Tweed to this day and is marked on maps.) It was nowhere near Catterick in Swaledale. Nor could Gwen Ystrad, fought against Pictish sea raiders, have been at Catterick, a long way from salt water. However, Professor Clancy has at least read the poems and thought about them, unlike another, who calls eulogies of some twenty or thirty lines 'a series of epic poems'.[54]

Having reviewed opinion on Gwen Ystrad from the nineteenth century to the twenty-first, we now take stock. Two points are clear. One is the neglect of some early comment. This has been repeatedly observed as regards Watson in 1926, but is also true of Jenny Rowland's comments in 1990 on Gwallawg's defence of 'Llan Llennawg', located at 'Staynlenok' near Millom. The second point goes back still further, to Thomas Stephens in 1852. It modifies his suggestion by seeking to show, not that Gwensteri was 'Gwen Ystrad', but that

---

[50] Toop 2011.
[51] Breeze 2012a.
[52] Charles-Edwards 2013, 365, 378–89.
[53] Clancy 2013.
[54] Halsall 2013, 23.

'Gwen Ystrad' was Gwensteri, so that Urien defended Rheged against Pictish raiders on the banks of the Winster. To argue this we need to consider textual criticism, place-name studies and physical geography, the last for its strategic implications in sixth-century Rheged.

Textual criticism is for once a simple matter. The scribe of the fourteenth-century Book of Taliesin copied beautifully the poems before him, faultlessly reproducing their accumulated scribal errors. He was paid to copy them (which he did to perfection), not understand them. Yet his insouciance has meant labour and frustration for scholars in the last century and a half. Nevertheless, his text being the very sink of corruption, we need not hesitate to emend unknown 'Gwen Ystrad' to known 'Gwensteri'.

This brings us to philology. *Gwensteri* is a curious form. Its history is this. The Winster rises on Brent Fell in the former Westmorland and flows 11 miles south to enter the estuary of the Kent near Meathop (Norse for 'raised ground in marshland'). Ekwall, relating the form to Norse *vinstri* ('left, and so the left-hand river'), dismissed McClure's 1910 suggestion of 'white river' (in the light of the Welsh for 'white' and Breton for 'water') as impossible, because the Winster 'has dark brown water'.[55] But he did not know about *Gwensteri*. McClure's 'white stream' is thus now thought possible, with the comment that 'whitish clay has been dredged from the river'.[56] There is an objection that Breton *steri* 'streams' otherwise has no known cognate in Insular Brittonic. Despite that, we may regard Winster as Celtic (and not Norse), like the neighbouring Kent (cf. Welsh *cu* (hound)), Leven (Welsh *llwyf* (elm)), Crake (Welsh *carrog* (torrent)), Duddon, and Mite (Welsh *muchudd* (jet-stone)).

Now for our last part. If we emend 'Gwen Ystrad' to *Gwensteri*, thereby turning the clock back to 1852, when Thomas Stephens (1821–1875) proposed that 'Gwen Ystrad' was Winsterdale, does this fit the evidence of the poetry? Let us look again at the translation above. There are three points. First, line six. J. P. Clancy translated it as 'Pictland's men, deadly war-bands'. In his 1968 edition, Ifor Williams notes Lloyd-Jones's implicit 'The men of Britain have come in hosts' to Gwen Ystrad. He himself offered 'The warriors of Britain wrought destructions in hosts'. But he admitted that the rare word *caffon*, taken in line twenty-two ('Waves washed the tails of their horses') as 'steeds', would indicate the enemy as Picts and not English, because the latter fought on foot.

If the enemy were Picts, this brings us to a second point. The poet refers continually to the sea. He declares, 'Like waves roaring harsh onto shore / I saw savage men in war-bands', which might, of course, be applied to warriors on moorland, but which is more apt for combat by salt water. The enemies

---

[55] Ekwall 1922, 190.
[56] Watts 2004, 686.

were aliens, 'border-crossing forces' slaughtered by Urien's men. He witnessed their surrender:

> At the ford I saw men stained with blood
> Downing arms before a grey-haired lord:
> They wished peace, for they found the way barred,
> Hands crossed, on the strand, cheeks pallid.
> Their lords wondered at Idon's rich wine;
> Waves washed the tails of their horses.
> I saw pillaging men blunted
> And blood spattering their garments.

Here again we hear of places by water. There are fighting men at a ford; they stand on a strand (*gro*, which is gravel by a river or shingle on a beach); their steeds are in water up to the knee; and their riders are pillagers, who have come like pirates for plunder, not territory. Perhaps more significant are lines following:

> I saw noble men about Urien
> When he cut down his foes in Llech Wen.

Llech Wen is 'white slab, white crag' (not 'Gwen's crag'), as with Harlech 'fair crag' in north Wales, from which Branwen in the twelfth-century *Mabinogion* tale beheld ships of the King of Ireland, who came to seek her hand.[57] The crag of the poem, scene of bloodier events, has not previously been identified. But it may have been Whitbarrow (white hill), three miles long and seven-hundred feet high, which overlooks the Winster from the east. Whitbarrow has crags at White Scar and elsewhere that are visible for miles; English Whitbarrow (white hill) translates Welsh *llech wen* (white crag) rather well. The proximity of Whitbarrow and the Winster is thus evidence for the poem's authenticity. It tends to confirm what Thomas Stephens suggested, that Urien defeated alien attackers in wetlands of the Winster.

The third point takes us from this battle poem to another by Taliesin, on Gwallawg. Though also martial, it does not describe a particular engagement. Like other Welsh verses, it lists and praises a warlord's triumphs up and down the land. The translation of 2002 cited above refers to conflict at Edinburgh, Bathgate and York, as well as 'a battle on the Winster, subduing the English'. It calls Gwallawg defender of 'delightful Llan Llennawg', which we take as the former 'Staynlenok', near Millom, 15 miles west of the Winster. A panegyric is

---

[57] Breeze 2009, 104.

not a military gazette, and Gwallawg's victories were perhaps less glorious than implied, so that Taliesin's claim of how torque-girded leaders from Dumbarton (on the Clyde) to Caer Garadawg (on the Wye) offered fealty to Gwallawg was no doubt at a remove from actuality. Yet the implications for south Cumbria as sixth-century battle-zone are clear enough. As for Lloyd-Jones's objection to the paean's *yg* (in), which is not used with hydronyms, unlike *ar* (on), this is easily countered. Later copyists would not recognize Gwensteri as a river name. To them it was merely one of a jumble of toponyms from the lost lands of the North. The point can be proved from Welsh annals on the battle of Brunanburh in 937. Earlier ones call it *ryfel Brun*, later ones *ymlad y Brune*, with the definite article.[58] Because rivers in Welsh (unlike English, where we speak of the Thames, the Aire and so on) are never referred to with the definite article, this shows *Brune* (the River Browney near Lanchester, eight miles from Durham) was no longer understood by Welsh scribes as a river name. Just as Welsh scribes forgot that *Brune* or Browney was a river, so too with *Gwinsteri* or Winster.

The conclusions of the above are evident. In the Taliesin debate, its analysis supports what Thomas Charles-Edwards calls the 'cheerfully constructive' side represented by John Koch, as against the negativism of Oliver Padel and Graham Isaac. We may agree with Watson in seeing the poem on Gwen Ystrad (better *Gwensteri* or, with two syllables, Old Welsh *Guenster*) as depicting Urien's defeat of a Pictish sea raid on Rheged. It will not have been on the shores of the Solway, as he thought, but further south, in the region south-east of Windermere and east of Grange-over-Sands. Dr Isaac's view that the poem is an eleventh-century forgery may be rejected. That trouble from the English might also be expected in this area is implied by another poem of Taliesin, to Gwallawg of Elmet.

Disputes on the authenticity of the 12 archaic poems in the Book of Taliesin have been going on merrily for a century and more. There is still, of course, much work to be done, on Taliesin's diction, language and metrics, as well as his toponyms and politics.[59] An obvious subject here is his other battle poem on Urien's massacre of English invaders at Argoed Llwyfain. The engagement may have been near the River Lyvennet, south of Penrith and so near the Roman road from the east coast via Stainmore. If this can be shown as probable, it will be further evidence for Urien's defence of territory in the North-West, some 30 miles north of Llech Wen (if correctly taken as the fell of Whitbarrow) and Gwensteri or the River Winster, Cumbria.

---

[58] Dumville 2005, 39.
[59] Haycock 2007, 6.

Now for a postscript. The material above appeared in 2015.[60] Since then have appeared two relevant articles. First is a lengthy study by Professor Sims-Williams, continuing his campaign against the earliest Welsh poems as supposedly of the late sixth or early seventh century, with the implication that they are later forgeries.[61] Second (and in complete contrast) is my account of Rheged. I derive its name from Latin *rece(p)tus* (retreat, refuge, place of shelter), an etymology which (after the paper was written) Professor David Dumville told him had been appeared (after a suggestion of Egerton Phillimore) in Morris-Jones's 1918 edition of Taliesin, but which was not taken on board by such later writers. It tends to confirm the realm ruled by Urien as centring on the area around Penrith and Appleby, sheltered on three sides by mountains. There is no reason to think that Urien ruled from Carlisle, although he clearly exercised authority up to the River Ayr in Scotland, where he fought troops from Strathclyde, as well as in the rest of Cumbria, north Lancashire (but not as far south as Rochdale, where the form has no direct link with 'Rheged') and north-west Yorkshire.[62]

So the debate initiated in 1918 by John Morris-Jones, continued thereafter by Ifor Williams and Kenneth Jackson against the doubts of Professor David Greene and Sir Thomas Parry, goes on in the twenty-first century. The question may yet soon be resolved. Analysis in previous chapters of the Twelve Battles of Arthur listed in *Historia Brittonum* places all but one of them in southern Scotland and Northumberland, and lets one reject Mount Badon as un-Arthurian. In a similar way, analysis of the toponyms in Taliesin's work also helps indicate their location, which will be in the later Westmorland and adjoining regions, with obvious implications for them as authentic writing of 590s or so.

---

[60] Breeze 2015b.
[61] Sims-Williams 2016.
[62] Breeze 2018c.

Chapter 5

603: CARNAGE AT '*DEGSASTAN*' BY WESTER DAWYCK, BORDERS

The Battle of 'Degsastan' was decisive for both Northumbria and Scotland. For the Northumbrians it began an ascendancy on its northern border which lasted until the Viking Age; for the Scots it was a crushing defeat, a seventh-century equivalent of Flodden Field or Culloden. Thanks to Bede, we know that it was fought in 603; we know too that in it, after bitter fighting, the Bernicians vanquished the Scots of Dál Riada. Yet, the conflict's whereabouts having been unknown, we here set out previous discussion of it, before offering fresh arguments for its location and the meaning of its name. If correct, they provide a solution to a problem debated by scholars since the late seventeenth century.

We start, as often, with Charles Plummer (1851–1927), who thought that the name *Degsastan* might actually be due to the battle, being a corruption of the Old English for 'at Aedán's stone'.[1] (The suggestion makes no sense, but is still significant. Prompted by *Egesan stane* in Abingdon versions of the *Anglo-Saxon Chronicle*, it shows how even speakers of Old English were baffled by the form.) Plummer elsewhere brought out the perplexity of his predecessors. Quoting W. F. Skene (1809–1892) and noting the philological objections to Dalston, near Carlisle, he took the place as 'Probably Dawston, in Liddesdale'. He also mentioned (as other proposals) Theekstone, north of Ripon, and Dissington, north-west of Newcastle.[2] No one remembers these. An older view appears in collections of Joseph Bosworth (1789–1876), which state 'DAWSTON or Dalston, Cumberland'.[3]

Even in the twentieth century, the conflict was still vaguely related to Dawstone (near Jedburgh) or Dalston (near Carlisle), as well as Dawston Rigg in Roxburghshire/Borders.[4] The last has thereafter ousted other contenders

---

[1] Plummer 1899, 18.
[2] Plummer 1896, II, 66.
[3] Toller 1898, 193–94.
[4] Rhys 1904, 159.

(on the principle that a bad suggestion is better than a worse one). We start with Anderson's version of Bede's text. 'In these times Ethelfrid, a most powerful king, and very eager for glory, reigned over the kingdom of the Northumbrians.' Than him 'no one among kings, after expelling or subduing the inhabitants, made more of their lands either tributary to the English nation or habitable by them', so that Bede applied Old Testament language to him, the king resembling Saul as a 'ravening wolf' which devoured prey and divided spoil. 'Wherefore Aidan, king of the Scots who dwell in Britain, was disturbed by his advance, and came against him with a huge and mighty army; but he was conquered, and fled away with few. For almost all his army was slain in a most renowned place which is called Degsastan; that is, Degsa stone.' Anderson listed references to the battle in medieval English sources, including William of Malmesbury and Henry of Huntingdon. On location, he suggested, 'Perhaps Dawstane, near Jedburgh'.[5] This, the 'Dawston, in Liddesdale' of Skene and Plummer, figures on maps as Dawston Burn (National Grid Reference (NGR) NY 5698), with a road under a disused railway viaduct in desolate country below Saughtree Fell (1,425 feet), 15 miles south-south-west of Jedburgh.

Sir John Lloyd (1861–1947) narrated in a stately manner the career of Æthelfrith. The king's aggressions, 'a most threatening movement', enabled him in 604 to annex Deira to Bernicia, putting him in 'an exceedingly strong position', so that north of the Humber he was 'without a rival'. Before that, in 603, 'he had been attacked by Aidan, king of the important Irish or "Scottish" colony which had established itself in Argyll, with a large army which probably included a contingent of Cymry from the region of the Clyde; but Aidan sustained a crushing defeat at Degsastán (The Stone of Degsa), probably Dawston at the head of Liddesdale.' Lloyd thought that the distinction 'achieved through this victory' encouraged the king 'soon after to lay his hands upon Deira', so that in the next decade he was strong enough to fight at Chester, killing the rulers of Powys and Rhos from east and north-east Wales.[6] Lloyd persuaded few as regards Strathclyde presence in the engagement, for obvious reasons. The battle is unnoticed in British sources, in contrast to those at Chester in 616, *Haethfelth* (south-east of Doncaster) in 633, Rowley Burn (near Hexham) in 634, *Maserfelth* (in the Welsh district of *Meisir*, and so east of Forden, Powys) in 642, or the *Uinued* (on the Went, north-west of Doncaster) in 655.

Professor William Watson of Edinburgh had informed remarks on the battle's Celtic dimension. He spoke of how in 603 'Aedán appears as head of a great confederate host', one of his followers being 'Mael-umae, son of

---

[5] Anderson 1908, 11.
[6] Lloyd 1911, 178–79.

Báetán mac Muirchertaigh' from Ireland, who slew Eanfrid, the Bernician king's brother. Watson observed on *Degsastan*, 'which Skene has identified with Dawstone in Liddesdale', that its result 'was finally reversed five hundred years later at Carham (1018)'. He added, 'Had Aedán been victorious, the result might well have been the political fusion of Urien's province [= Rheged] and even Lothian with Dál Riata at that time.'[7]

After a Scot, a Welshman. In his great edition of Aneirin's *Gododdin*, Sir Ifor Williams related *Degsastan* to this series of laments for North British warriors wiped out in an attack on the English at Catterick (in Yorkshire). He thought that the attack predated the battle. If Aidan was roundly defeated in 603, leaving 'almost all his men dead on the field', then a Gododdin ruler in its aftermath would hardly send another army to attack the English.[8] Max Förster (1869–1954) of Munich made a gallant attempt to derive *Degsa* from reconstructed Celtic personal name in *Dagissa-*.[9] It is ingenious but unconvincing. Förster being a great scholar, we yet infer that *Degsa* is not English. It must be Celtic. We shall return to this. In careful analysis of chronology, Levison gave the year of *Degsastan* as 603.[10] A standard atlas puts *Degsastan* with a query in Liddesdale, on the frontier of Rheged and Bernicia.[11]

Kenneth Jackson cited Förster's etymology, but observed that 'the etymology is very uncertain'.[12] One sees why. Personal names in *Dago-* are known in Gaulish but not British, and nothing corresponds with Förster's supposed *Dagissa-* in Welsh, Cornish or Breton nomenclature. The derivation must be dropped. Scepticism of a different kind was offered by Peter Hunter Blair. He made important observations. Bede's sources for the conflict, whether English or Celtic, are unknown. His *locus celeberrimus* points to stories current in his day, but his precision on the year implies more than oral tradition. The *Anglo-Saxon Chronicle*'s D and E texts (from Abingdon) mention one thing, which Bede does not, on how Hering, son of Hussa, led troops to the engagement. Hering is unidentified, but Hussa figures in the ninth-century *Historia Brittonum*. Unfortunately, the statement leaves it unclear whose side Hering was on. As for the Irish annals, they state that Máil Umai killed Æthelfrith's brother Eanfrid, of whom English sources know nothing. He cannot be Æthelfrith's son Eanfrid, because he was alive thirty years later. Important too are Hunter Blair's remarks on place. The first person to propose Dawston

[7] Watson 1926, 130, 156.
[8] Williams 1938, xlii.
[9] Förster 1941, 809.
[10] Levison, 1946, 272.
[11] Rees 1951, plate 20.
[12] Jackson 1953, 612.

was Edmund Gibson (1669–1748), antiquary and librarian (and thereafter Bishop of London), in his 1692 edition of the *Anglo-Saxon Chronicle*. Hunter Blair had dusty views of this youthful scholar's gloss, as also Förster's more sophisticated reasoning. 'To anyone acquainted with this wild and barren fell country, Förster's picture of English invaders settling here and adopting a place-name from the defeated British will not be convincing.' He concluded that, for modern writers, in words from John Smith's 1722 edition of Bede, *hic locus, Bedae seculo tam celebris, hodie ignotus est.*[13]

Jackson, on 'Aedhán son of Gabhrán, king of Scottish Dál Riada', mentions his Britishness and anti-Britishness. Despite having a son called Arthur and grandson called Rígullón, where both forms are British, Aedán fell out with the Britons of Strathclyde, leading a costly raid on their capital at Dumbarton. Hence his reputation for treachery in later Welsh tradition.[14] Wainwright remarked on how Aedán, 'a mighty king, aggressive if not invincible', could have made the Scots the dominant people of north Britain had he not met his match at *Degsastan*, 'dubiously identified with Dawston in Liddesdale'. He added that, even if Förster had resolved the philological objections here, 'the positive evidence in its favour remains slight'.[15] Campbell treated *Degsa* as an Old English weak noun, which in Northumbrian dialect would lose -*n* in the genitive singular. Hence *Degsastan*, not the *Degsanstan* expected in other dialects.[16] He passed by Förster's analysis of the form. With careful reasoning, Jackson showed how Edinburgh, capital of the Gododdin, fell to the Northumbrians in 638, long after *Degsastan*.[17] Despite a Gaelic Armageddon on their borders, the Gododdin remained independent of their menacing English neighbours for more than a generation.

Hunter Blair, ever hostile to Dawston in Liddesdale, declared the site of battle as 'still renowned in Bede's lifetime, but now lost'. Aedán's headquarters are, in contrast, well known. His capital was Dunadd (NGR NR 8393), a hillock two miles north of the Crinan Canal.[18] Dunadd appears on the Ordnance Survey historical map for the period, as does *Degsastan*-Dawston, doubts notwithstanding.[19]

Isabel Henderson, giving attention to Celtic sources, quotes Adomnán's life of St Columba for the death of Domingart, son of Aedán, on a 'rout' in

---

[13] Hunter Blair 1954, 137–72.
[14] Jackson 1955, 77–88.
[15] Wainwright 1955, 1–53.
[16] Campbell 1959, 189.
[17] Jackson 1959b, 35–42.
[18] Hunter Blair 1963, 201.
[19] *Map of Britain in the Dark Ages*, 1966.

England, perhaps *Degsastan,* perhaps another bloodletting. As for the battle itself, its site 'has yet to be identified'.[20] Professor Kirby still said 'probably in Liddesdale' and, better, noted how North British royal genealogies begin to terminate in the early seventh century, thereby confirming Bede's picture of Bernicia as 'a powerful military state', the 'spearhead of the Anglian attack on the north'.[21] In the Celtic camp, Bannerman cited evidence from Irish saga for a military alliance between the Dál Riada and the Dál nAraide of east Ulster.[22] Colgrave and Mynors spoke of Bernician 'conquest of the Irish tribes to the north', which is misleading. The Dál Riada were roundly defeated; but not conquered. These editors further related Bede's *gloriae cupidissimus* to Old English *domgeorn* (eager for glory), thinking that the 'whole chapter may well have been influenced by some lost heroic poem', resembling the tenth-century *Battle of Brunanburh* or *Battle of Maldon,* and observed that the battlefield is 'not certainly known, though it is usually identified with Dawston Rigg in Liddesdale'.[23] All three statements may be rejected: on conquest of Irish 'tribes'; on a vernacular poem as Bede's source; and on Dawston, a seventeenth-century bad guess. Hunter Blair modified his scepticism on location to position Æthelfrith's defeat of Aedán 'probably somewhere to the south of the Firth of Forth'.[24]

Kenneth Jackson, following Hunter Blair on *Degsastán* as at a site 'unknown', set out the conflict's historical context, referring to Aedán's alliance with 'an Irish prince of the powerful northern Uí Néill' and to evidence for a son of Hussa as 'captain of the army'.[25] Leslie Alcock said much on it, though with a less sure touch, including (unfortunately) the equation 'probably Dawston in Liddesdale'. He made the startling observation on that Æthelfrith 'was not himself involved in the battle', on the basis of the *Chronicle's* statement concerning Hering, son of Hussa. However, his comment on the distance from Dunadd to Dawston (120 'crow-miles', but further by land) is a welcome glimpse of fact.[26] It reminds us of the logistical difficulties of moving and supplying thousands of troops, whether by sea or by land. Sir Frank Stenton was, as usual, to the point. Old English *Degsastane* should give *Daystone,* not *Dawston.* Identification of the place of slaughter was hence 'best left an open question'.[27]

[20] Henderson 1967, 49, 50.
[21] Kirby 1967, 24, 25.
[22] Bannerman 1968, 1–11.
[23] Colgrave and Mynors 1969, 116n1, 117n4.
[24] Jackson 1969, 10.
[25] Hunter Blair 1970, 19.
[26] Alcock 1971, 131, 324, 338.
[27] Stenton 1971, 77n2.

On the Celtic side, the Maeluma, son of Báetán of the Cenél nEógain, killed in 603 is described as son of a King of Tara in the early 570s.[28] Aedán's war was waged by a grand alliance. Marjorie Anderson commented on when the hosts of Dál Riada were annihilated, but not where.[29] F. J. Byrne styles Máel Umai, Aedán's ally in the conflict, as 'son of the so-called high-king Báetán mac Muirchetaig'.[30] John Morris wrote of Aedán that, 'reinforced by the King of Ireland's brother, he was able to lead a large force to help the British a second time against the English', only to encounter 'crushing and decisive defeat'.[31] There are three errors in that quotation, and the paragraph from which they come contains more. John Bannerman thereafter devoted a long passage to the event, which despite 'numerous attempts' was unlocated, though probably 'within the limits of Northumbrian authority'. He believed that Aedán may have abdicated or been deposed following the disaster; and, if Hering, son of Hussa, was Aedán's guide, it points to a meeting of armies far from Dál Riada and within Bernicia. Bannerman (having ignored the British territories sandwiched between Gael and Angle) downplayed the notion of Aedán's coming to the help of the Britons. He commented further on how Aedán, most unusually for a Gaelic leader, figures in medieval Welsh tradition, but not with praise.[32] Finberg described the spot where armies clashed as 'not certainly identifiable, but evidently in Anglian territory'.[33]

Archibald Duncan summed up Aedán as suffering 'the fate of others who stumble in a freebooting career' by (apparently) losing his office. 'Behind Adamnan's pious Aedán consecrated by Columba's hand lies a tough opportunist, enemy of all his neighbours and master of most of them.' This unscrupulous political operator's Waterloo 'has never been satisfactorily identified, though one would expect it to survive as the site of a monolith and to have the name Daystone'. (A perceptive remark. The 'monolith' can be seen to this day.) The attack 'was probably a raid for plunder by the Scots', seemingly 'led there by the son of a previous Bernician king; it was certainly a famous victory, for it found its way into the Irish annals'.[34] Hunter Blair commented that, 'despite the efforts of many ingenious and learned men', the field of conflict is unknown, although it was surely between Bamburgh and the Firth of Forth.[35] Elsewhere he placed the engagement to shortly after the catastrophic attack of

---

[28] Mac Niocaill 1972, 79.
[29] Anderson 1973, 13n55.
[30] Byrne 1973, 111.
[31] Morris 1973, 183.
[32] Bannerman 1974, 86–89.
[33] Finberg 1974, 24.
[34] Duncan 1975, 44, 60.
[35] Hunter Blair 1976, 41, 46.

the Gododdin on *Catraeth* or Catterick, a raid known solely from Aneirin's elegies for the fallen. Hunter Blair added that the Scots did not renew pressure on Northumbria until the ninth century, when they came close to bringing their border 'as far south as the Tees'.[36] Duncan and Hunter Blair saw *Degsastan* as a monumental victory. Its direct effects lasted for more than two hundred and sixty years.

Croft Dickinson did more than relate the 'complete but costly' Anglian victory of 603 to Northumbrian expansion northwards between then and their vanquishing by the Picts in 685. He stressed loot. The raid was carried out for booty: weapons, coins, silver, perhaps cattle. He drew attention as well to documents from Gaelic Scotland which let us estimate how many men and ships a king required for such a campaign.[37] The information helps us a little to imagine the situation of generals in the spring of 603, planning a summer campaign. Dr Bromwich gave a useful synopsis of the ill-fame which Aedán, son of Gabran, gained in Welsh triads and annals, together with the interesting view that the British attack on *Catraeth* and Scots-Irish defeat at *Degsastan* were identical.[38] Now, the two places cannot have been the same. But we may recall that events at Catterick hardly postdated 603–604, when the Bernicians vanquished the Scots and Irish and then annexed Deira, gaining an unassailable position, so that any North British assault would have been madness. It may thus be that the advance on Catterick was simultaneous with the *Degsastan* campaign, on the principle of a two-pronged attack used with effect at Stamford Bridge and Hastings in 1066. While a Scots-Irish army made for Bamburgh in the north of Bernicia, one of the Gododdin made for Catterick on its southern frontier. Such a hypothesis accords with details in Welsh poetry on the year-long planning for the march on Catterick and the lack of references to North British participation at *Degsastan*. It would date the heroic British defeat at Catterick to the summer of 603, with Aneirin's elegies to the dead being composed immediately after.

Professor Sawyer, however, observed that the crushing humiliation of 603 was soon followed by good relations between Northumbria and Dál Riada. Like Croft Dickinson, he regarded the invasion as a raid for plunder, not a bid for territorial gain.[39] English sources for it were set out by Dorothy Whitelock, who cited Förster as defender of the Liddesdale school.[40] On Bede's source, Archibald Duncan made two suggestions. He saw it as having led to confusion

---

[36] Hunter Blair 1977, 44–45.
[37] Dickinson 1977, 26, 47, 48.
[38] Bromwich 1978b, 264–66, 543.
[39] Sawyer 1978, 25.
[40] Whitelock 1979, 159, 658.

between the Scots-Irish defeat at *Degsastan* in 603 and Welsh defeat at Chester in 616. He took the sources as 'a British Latin lament in the manner of Gildas for the miseries inflicted upon monks, written probably at Bangor[-on-Dee].'[41] This is speculative, to say the least. But he may be right in thinking Bede's source a British Latin one. It would account for the curious form *Degsastan*, where the first element is not English. Wallace-Hadrill, who cited Duncan's opinions in neutral terms, was negative on what C. W. Jones said of *Degsastan* in his *Saints' Lives and Chronicles* of 1947, such as the field of battle's being close to Jarrow (hence *celeberrimo*), with the stone a local monument. Wallace-Hadrill also eyed coldly Colgrave's postulating a 'lost heroic poem' as a source. Bede probably had little more than an annal.[42] A surprise on the persistence of tradition comes from the eleventh-century *Mabinogion* tale of Culhwch and Olwen. It mentions Maylwys mab Baedan, who is none other than the Irish warrior Máel Umai mac Baitán, his name remembered by a storyteller in south-west Wales nearly five centuries after his martial career.[43]

Nick Higham thinks that Dál Riada's attack on Æthelfrith shows how the 'protection' of this 'overking' was active as far north as Strathclyde.[44] Michael Swanton, giving the Liddesdale location, nevertheless cites Hunter Blair's scepticism of 1954.[45] Michael Lapidge reproduced unquestioningly the corrupt reading 'Degsastan'; André Crépin thought possible the impossible location 'dans le Liddisdale au nord de Carlisle' and reproduced Plummer's absurd etymology.[46] Nick Higham then ventured into philology. He opines this on *Degsastan*. 'Although it arguably contains as its first element a Scottish personal name, the suffix implies that the place-name was formed in Old English, which suggests that it may have been within Northumbria, at some stage at least.'[47] One would like to know the 'Scottish personal name' which Professor Higham had in mind. In similar vein, the late Proinsias Mac Cana stated that 'according to at least one version of the event' Mael Umai killed Theobald, Æthelfrith's brother. No version of anything does this. Professor Mac Cana confused the Theobald of Bede's narrative with the Eanfrid of Irish annals.[48] Yet there is a victory in a recent historical atlas. Unlike those of 1951 and 1966 cited above, it does not mark *Degsastan* in Liddesdale or anywhere else.[49]

---

[41] Duncan 1981, 1–42.
[42] Wallace-Hadrill 1988, 47–48.
[43] Bromwich and Evans 1992, 69.
[44] Higham 1995, 77.
[45] Swanton 1996, 21n9.
[46] Crépin and Lapidge 2005a, 264.
[47] Higham 2006, 236.
[48] Mac Cana 2007, 17–45.
[49] Koch 2007, map 21.2

Despite that, the Edinburgh History of Scotland gives the field of battle as 'possibly in Liddesdale or Lauderdale', a reason for the latter and novel choice not being given.[50] As a reminder of traditional views is a history of Celtic Christianity published only in 2009. It was written in Valladolid, at the English College, by the rector Philip Perry (1720–1774). His grasp of the material is clear from his comment on 'the bloody Battle of Degsastane, fought in 603 against Edilfrid, the fierce king of the Bernicians, who gave Aidan so complete and terrible an overthrow, that he only escaped with a few of his soldiers. "And from that day to this," adds Bede, i.e., during a whole century and more, "none of the Scottish kings has ever dared to invade the English territories".' Perry's view of the battle resembles that of later historians, but is more crisply put and, after nearly two and a half centuries, has arrived in print.[51]

Some real thought on the matter comes from Tim Clarkson. The spot is 'not identifiable today'. The equating of *Degsastan* and Dawston 'originated as a philological guess' first made in 1692 by Edmund Gibson. The stone itself 'was either a monolith of natural origin (such as a large glacial boulder) or a standing-stone erected in prehistoric times.' There is nothing like that near Dawston. If we are ever to find where it was, 'we may tentatively suggest Lothian or Lanarkshire as possible zones of conflict' between Scot and Angle.[52] In a handbook on Bede, *Degsastan* appears briefly, but not by name.[53] Celtic traditions on it are now set out accurately and conveniently.[54] In an archaeological paper the place is described as 'unidentified, but, given the two protagonists, presumably in the west'.[55] Aedán figures in a detailed study, without mention of the catastrophe which did for him.[56] Yet we hear elsewhere that the 'battle at *Catraeth* is probably neither that of *Degsastan* nor that of *Gwen Ystrad*'.[57] We can be bolder. The first will be Catterick in Yorkshire, the last the River Winster in south Cumbria, but *Degsastan*, we shall now argue, was far north of these, being in Tweedsdale, Scotland.

Since this paper was written in 2013, the following accounts have appeared. Thomas Charles-Edwards, doubting whether the Bernicians 'defeated a major attack by the king of Dál Riata' in 603, thinks that it was perhaps in 599, when their prince Domangart died 'in English battle-slaughter'.[58] An interesting

---

[50] Fraser 2009, 141.
[51] Carrera and Carrera 2009, 185.
[52] Clarkson 2010, 120, 114–15.
[53] Thacker 2010, 170–89.
[54] Sims-Williams 2011, 173.
[55] Clark 2011, 113–28.
[56] Dumville 2011, 41–52.
[57] Clancy 2013, 153–75.
[58] Charles-Edwards 2013, 345.

point. Professor Halsall, in a book which cannot be recommended, notes the conflict as usually located 'near Dawston Burn in Liddesdale'.[59] Tim Clarkson (in a survey of the period) does not mention it by name, but he does comment on how the British kingdoms centred on Dumbarton, Penrith (of Rheged), and Edinburgh (of the Gododdin), escaped Bernician onslaughts 'and seemingly survived Edwin's reign too'.[60] Schustereder believes that because of the engagement the Irish were 'driven off the island of Great Britain', which is not true, for they still occupied Argyll and beyond.[61] Also untrue is Barbara Yorke's claim, citing this chapter of Bede, that its author took the Bernician 'attack in 603 on the British clergy' as 'an examply of devine ordained vengeance'.[62] Not so. Professor Yorke has confused the victory of 603 with the Northumbrian one at Chester in 613 or 616. Hick Higham now refers to Irish traditions of 603.[63] The Irish did not forget this bloodbath or how the English (as even Bede admitted) paid dear for their triumph. But no word on location.

Our survey has extended from a tenth-century Abingdon scribe of the *Anglo-Saxon Chronicle*, who took *Degsastan* as 'the *Egesan stan*', to Professor Higham in the twenty-first. Now we come to our last part, on where those Scottish-Irish and English armies met. Commentators never put themselves in the position of Aedán and his generals. Yet a simple map shows how, for an attack on the coast of north Northumberland from Argyll, there are two possible routes. One runs along the Antonine Wall and across the Lothian plain; the other passes Glasgow, and then up Clydesdale (with its Roman road) to the gap by Biggar (NGR NT 0437) and then down the Tweed valley. By that route an enemy would reach Northumberland's northern plains and the Bernician seats of power at Yeavering (NGR NT 9230), Milfield (NGR NT 9433), and Bamburgh (NGR NU 1835). A third and southern route by way of Carlisle and Hadrian's Wall is too long and slow. An attacker would lose the element of surprise. In short, the Tweed valley offers the sole east-west corridor in the region between the two Walls.[64] The point was made again in the railway age, when the one east-west line between Lothian and the Tyne Gap followed the Tweed, from Carstairs to Tweedmouth via Biggar, Peebles, and Galashiels.

If we then look at maps of Tweedsdale, we find abundant hillcamps, Roman forts, castles, and peel towers marked as proof of ancient insecurity. But we also find east of the Biggar gap near Drumelzier a monolith (NGR NT

[59] Halsall 2013, 23.
[60] Clarkson 2014, 33.
[61] Schustereder 2015, 179.
[62] Yorke 2016, 237–57.
[63] Higham 2018, 211.
[64] *Map of Roman Britain*, 1956.

1335) standing in meadowland.[65] Could this stone be *Degsastan*? There is certainly a case. It is conspicuous above the river on an obvious route along Clyde and Tweed. The meadows around it would be marshland in the seventh century, so that armies on this strategic corridor through the Southern Uplands would be confined to strips of dry land on each side of the river. As a locale (by a ford in the Tweed?) where a Bernician army might bottle up a foe advancing from the west, this part of Tweedsdale makes sense, as Liddesdale does not.

If the Drumelzier standing stone is accepted as a candidate for *Degsastan*, the next problem is the text. *Degsa* is not English, but no Welsh or Cumbric form has been found to explain it. (It will not be Gaelic, because no Gael settled by the Tweed until four centuries after Aedán's defeat.) The first element is suspicious. It may be corrupt. Even if Bede's text is as pure as one by Gibbon or Macaulay, it still has errors in non-English forms, some of them due to Bede's sources. Here are four of them. Book one of *Historia Ecclesiastica* tells the story of 'Elafius', a man of authority in fifth-century Britain, whose paralytic son was cured by St Germanus of Auxerre. 'Elafius' is not Celtic but Greek, the correct reading *Elafus* (from *elaphos* 'deer') occurring as a variant in Constantius's life of St Germanus, Bede's source. Book two of his *Historia* mentions 'Dommoc', the Roman fort (now washed away by the sea) of Walton Castle (NGR TM 3235) near Felixstowe, Suffolk. In the seventh century it was a monastery and seat of a bishop. 'Dommoc' is corrupt. The name will be *Civitas Domnoc*, due to an Irishman called *Domnoc*, like the Domnoc or Modomnoc (= 'My Domnoc') taught by St David.[66] It has nothing to do with Dunwich (also washed away by the sea) in north-east Suffolk, where *Dunwich* 'beach sheds' is purely English (as Professor Richard Coates has shown). Book three of Bede's history notoriously has the account of St 'Ninnian', where the form is accepted as a misreading of *Uinniau* or Finnian. The real 'Ninnian' was none other than St Finnian (d. 579), founder of the community at Moville, near Newtownards in Northern Ireland.[67] Book three refers also to 'Paegnalaech', the monastery where Bishop Tuda of Lindisfarne was buried in 664. This will be *Uaegnalaech* (meadow stream), where the first element relates to the British form giving Welsh *gwaun* (meadow).[68] The mistake arose because the Anglo-Saxon grapheme 'wynn resembles P', and has been read as one. Once the error of a single letter is recognized, we may locate *Uaegnalaech* at Wawne (NGR TA 0936), north of Hull, Yorkshire. At this spot there will have been

---

[65] *Peeblesshire*, 1967.
[66] Plummer 1925, 217.
[67] Edmonds 2011, 8–9.
[68] Cullen 2008, 95–100.

a previously unknown Northumbrian monastery, where the bones of Bishop Tuda lie.

Recalling these four instances, we may also take *Degsastan* as corrupt. The first element being neither English nor Gaelic but Cumbric, we may seek a parallel in Welsh. If we do, we find an unexpected solution. The one form that tallies is *Degui*, the Old Welsh spelling of *Dewi* or David. It is known from place names. *Lann Degui Cilpedec* is Kilpeck (the 'peck' ultimately from Latin *pedica* meaning 'snare') and *Lann Deugui* is Much Dewchurch. Both are near Hereford and have the Old Welsh for *Llanddewi* 'church enclosure of Dewi, church of David'.[69] *Degui* occurs too in Asser's life of Alfred, referring to St Davids in West Wales.[70] Lotivy in Brittany is Old Breton *Loc Deugui* (holy place of Dewi).[71] Further references to Old Welsh *Degui* and its treatment as *Dewi* in English occur in a note on the name.[72] These Celtic spellings of 'Dewi' as *De(u)gui* allow emendation of *Degsa*, which nobody has made sense of, to *Degui*. The battle will apparently have been fought at the stone of a Briton known as *Degui* (David). The termination -*ui* here having three vertical strokes, it was not difficult for an English scribe to misread the first as minuscule *s* and the two latter as *a*. Bede's reading not only has symptoms of Old Welsh or, rather, Old Cumbrian spelling, but of Welsh or Cumbrian minuscule script.[73] We must also make clear, without going into details of Celtic sound changes and spelling, that Old Welsh and so Old Cumbrian *Degui* were pronounced like modern *Dewi*, with a short vowel. The spelling in 'g' is not historical, but analogous, like that of *Osguid* for English *Oswy* in *Annales Cambriae*.[74] There is another reason why we should read *Degui* 'Dewi, David' and not *Degsa*. Proof that many Britons were called after Israel's royal prophet and psalmist comes from Dewsbury, Yorkshire. This Victorian mill-town has medieval origins. It appears in Domesday Book, and its name means 'Dewi's stronghold'.[75] If there was a Dewi in pre-Norman Yorkshire, there might have been a Dewi in seventh-century North Britain.

Even if it is accepted that the Drumelzier stone is in the right place for our military confrontation, and that a reading *Degui lapis* (Asser's text shows *Degui* as undeclined in medieval Latin) is coherent as *Degsa lapis* is not, why should we think that name and place coincide? Is it not unfortunate that the toponym

[69] Evans 1893, 275, 276.

[70] Stevenson 1904, 65, 66.

[71] Harris 1940, 74.

[72] Dickins 1963, 206–209.

[73] Denholm-Young 1964, plate 7.

[74] Morris 1980, 87.

[75] Watts 2004, 186.

should have vanished from Tweedsdale? Perhaps it has not. Downstream from the stone are Wester Dawyck, Dawyck House (with old lime-trees and silver firs), ruined Dawyck Bank and Easter Dawyck. The earliest record for them is *Dawik* in 1501–1502. We are told that 'the quest for an etymology is highly speculative', because the sole candidates for the first element are Old English *da* 'doe, female deer' and *dawe* 'crow-like bird, jackdaw', with the latter seemingly unrecorded in English toponyms.[76] So another way out is possible. *Dawick* is perhaps not 'doe farm' or 'jackdaw farm' at all, but 'Dewi's farm', being named after its British owner, like Dewsbury (Dewi's fortified place) in Yorkshire. If *Dawick* is 'Dewi's farm' (with Scots lowering of the vowel, as in *Dauvit* against English *David*), then the monolith less than two miles from Western Dawyck might have been *Degui stan* ('Dewi's stone) (= 'Degsastan'), much as Davidstow in north-east Cornwall was formerly *Dewestowe* (Dewi's 'stow', Dewi's holy place).[77] Stones were often linked with a personal name. Examples up and down England include Allerston, Axton, Brixton (in inner London), Cuddlestone, Keston, Keystone and Tilson.[78] Nothing surprising, then, in a Dewi's stone on the banks of the Tweed.

Our proposal may be tested. A battle as bloody as that in 603 would leave thousands dead. Their bones may yet be found in Drumelzier parish, as also remains of their spears, swords, helmets, shields and other gear. If they are, and can be dated to about 600, it will confirm our philological and historical reasoning. They will show the deadly attraction of the royal palaces at Yeavering and Milfield, the first of which has (in the size and constructional techniques of its halls) fulfilled 'the expectations aroused by *Beowulf*.[79] Their gold and silver enticed a Scots-Irish army to its doom.

If the above arguments are sound, we may believe that, on a summer day in 603, bodies of Irish, Scot, and Angle lay slaughtered in fields by the Tweed, near the standing stone of Drumelzier. The action took place neither in English territory nor in Western Scotland, but in that of the Gododdin. A massive Scots-Irish force had come from Dunadd (NGR NR 8393) and Dunollie (NGR NM 8531), some on foot, some perhaps sailing across the Firth of Forth to Troon or Ayr, where a Roman road led west to upper Clydesdale, but all intent on English plunder. Æthelfrith knew they were coming. Informed by spies and scouts, he advanced to forestall them. The result was bloody but conclusive. Æthelfrith sat more firmly in the seat of power than ever; the preparations for Northumbria's three-century tenure of southern Scotland

---

[76] Nicolaisen 2002, 102.
[77] Padel 1988, 77.
[78] Gelling 1978, 186–87.
[79] Rahtz 1976, 49–98.

could go ahead; a hundred years later, Bede could vaunt that, since then, no king of Scots had dared to challenge Northumbria's ascendency. In short, *Deguistan* or 'Degsastan' had consequences which to this day affect British politics, languages and society; and we may bid farewell to the notion current since 1692 that *Degsastan* had anything to do with Dawston, Liddesdale.

Chapter 6

613: CHESTER AND THE MASSACRE OF WELSH MONKS

The Battle of Chester, dated by some to 613 (although others prefer 615), and (preceding it) the Northumbrian massacre of monks from Bangor-is-Coed were forgotten neither by the victors nor the vanquished. Almost from the day that it was fought, there have been English and Welsh accounts of the conflict. Among the Welsh this includes Geoffrey of Monmouth (d. 1155), Charles Edwards (1628–1691?) and Theophilus Evans (1693–1767). The second (as a Welsh patriot) claimed that native princes fought back, killing more than a thousand of their foes and thereby avenging the 'blood of the monks' (*gwaed y myneich*). [1] The third (as both Welsh patriot and Protestant) asserting that those monks differed from later monks, being devout men who served God 'in spirit and truth' (*mewn yspryd a gwirionedd*). [2] Inventions on the day are repeated by a nineteenth-century topographer, according to whom St Augustine warned how the Britons 'would speedily find death by swords of those to whom they had refused to preach the word of life', and how this came true, for the English slaughtered over a thousand monks of Bangor and then 'entirely destroyed the monastery, and committed its valuable library to the flames'. [3]

The subject of this paper is, however, not old legends but modern discussion, especially of a mysterious king 'Cetula' who fell in the battle. Plummer quoted an Irish annal on the Northumbria triumph: *Cecidit solon mac conain rex Bretannorum et cedula rex cecidit*. He identified the first as Selyf ap Cynan, king of Powys, yet confessed 'who Cedula was I am unable to say'. [4] He was followed on the engagement as in 616, with much other comment, including a remark on the Irish annalist's description of Selyf as *rex Bretannorum* as perhaps indicating that he was 'over-king of the Kymry'. [5] The conflict was described in

---

[1] Edwards 1948, 32.
[2] Evans 1961, 211.
[3] Lewis 1844, 67.
[4] Plummer 1896, II, 77.
[5] Rhys 1904, 126–27.

sober terms by Sir John Lloyd. He remarked that even Bede admitted the heavy Northumbrian losses. Lloyd added that Selyf ap Cynan, as ruler of Powys, was a 'natural defender of the Valley of the Dee' but that Gwynedd took no part in the fighting. He said nothing on 'Cetula'.[6] Hugh Williams did not mention the battle, yet did reject the notion 'first expressed by Henry VIII's antiquary John Leland' that the fifth-century heretic Pelagius came from Bangor-is-Coed.[7] A. H. Williams followed Lloyd in observing how Cadfan of Gwynedd (whose tombstone at Llangadwaladr on Anglesey shows dynastic aspirations) was probably not at Chester and how the battle foreshadowed a division between the Britons of Wales and the North Britons.[8]

In the 1950s, Rees plotted the cantrefs of Wales, including that of Rhos, which once occupied the whole coast between the Conway and Clwyd estuaries, including the stronghold at Degannwy, near Llandudno.[9] The relevance of this will be made clear below. Jackson pointed out that we cannot know what brought the Northumbrians so far south to fight an enemy whose territory did not border their own.[10] H. M. Chadwick, taking Selyf ap Cynan as British commander at Chester, regarded Powys as covering the entire region between the outlets of the Severn and the Dee.[11] Norah Chadwick posited a common written source behind Bede's narrative and the Welsh and Irish annals.[12] Revision came in the 1960s, with Loyn speaking of the raid as 'something of an isolated incident', the north-west not being colonized by the English until the later seventh century.[13] Nora Chadwick later wrote a full account of the conflict, mentioning the King Cetula who died there with Selyf ap Cynan but without saying who he was.[14] Hunter Blair called the English victory 'the outcome of a passing foray into British lands', for a while safe from English occupation.[15] Sir Idris Foster gave a version of Taliesin's supposed poem to Cynan Garwyn, whose son Selyf died at Chester.[16] A Bangor scholar was more pessimistic than Hunter Blair. She stated that, when the onslaught came, 'there was none amongst the Britons to support Selyf ap Cynan; his father, Cynan Garwyn, had been all too busy in sowing hatred (*ym rhy ddiwyd*

---

[6] Lloyd 1911, 181.
[7] Williams 1912, 200.
[8] Williams 1941, 78.
[9] Rees 1951, plate 28.
[10] Jackson 1953, 213–15.
[11] Chadwick 1954.
[12] Chadwick 1958.
[13] Loyn 1962, 9.
[14] Chadwick 1963.
[15] Hunter Blair 1963, 202.
[16] Foster 1965.

yn hau hadau casineb)' so that 'Powys was completely conquered', with the death of its king Selyf.[17] We shall yet show that Selyf was not alone; for 'Cetula' was his ally.

At this point we come to Bartrum, who in 1966 edited a genealogy of the rulers of Rhos, including a certain Catwal or Gadwal, great-grandson of the Cynlas savaged by Gildas in 536, whose citadel (as Gildas well knew, for he translated its name as 'receptaculum ursi') was the hillfort of Dinarth, near Colwyn Bay.[18] We shall come back to this Cadwal. Pennar Davies (1911–1996), poet-theologian and prisoner of conscience, saw the Bangor monks as patriot-martyrs (like him), who were 'fervent for victory over Britain or at least for the freedom and security of the Welsh (*neu o leiaf dros ryddid a diogelwch y Cymry*)'.[19] Like Charles Edwards and Theophilus Evans, he was stirred to indignation at what happened to Welshmen on that far-off day. Kirby, taking the battle as a Northumbrian show of force and a presage, commented on how pedigrees of Rheged and other North British kingdoms began to fade out in those years.[20] The poem to Cynan Garwyn, father of the valiant but doomed Selyf, was edited by Sir Ifor Williams.[21] Colgrave and Mynors observed of what Bede robustly called a 'great slaughter of that nation of heretics' that Chester remained desolate for nearly three centuries, until King Alfred rebuilt its walls.[22]

For writers of the 1970s, we start with Joseph Clancy's useful translation of the poem on Selyf's father. The bard refers to Cynan's slaughter of fellow Britons in Gwent, Anglesey, Ceredigion (at Crug Dyfed, east of Cardigan) and Cornwall, and declares, 'pathetic princes / Cringe before Cynan!'[23] If half of this is true, small wonder that Cynan Garwyn was called 'all too busy in sowing hatred', creating fatal difficulties for his son. Hunter Blair referred to the Northumbrian atrocity before the battle and the defeat of 'certain rulers from northern Wales', without saying who they were.[24] Alcock wrote of a clash of kingdoms, observing how it was not on Gwynedd but on Powys that the blow fell, although we do not know whether the Northumbrians intended merely an 'extended looting expedition' or had a greater strategic purpose. Nor can we say if Chester 'retained any administrative or military function at this date'. There is in any case 'no evidence for land-taking or settlement'

---

[17] Roberts 1965, 19–21.
[18] Bartrum 1966, 10.
[19] Davies 1966, 66.
[20] Kirby 1967, 24–25.
[21] Williams 1968, 1.
[22] Colgrave and Mynors 1969, 140–41.
[23] Clancy 1970, 23–24.
[24] Hunter Blair 1970, 81.

by the English after their triumph.[25] Sir Frank Stenton, in judicial mode, remarked that modern writers find a significance in the attack which Bede did not, and that there is no adequate reason for attributing the division of the British kingdoms to defeat at Chester.[26] Sir Ifor Williams as editor rightly noted this, as also Saunders Lewis's doubts on Taliesin's supposed poem to Cynan Garwyn.[27]

In contrast was John Morris, stating very strangely that the Northumbrians there 'defeated the combined forces of Gwynedd, Powys, and the lowland Cornovii', and thereby 'severed Wales from the Pennines'.[28] This surely prompted Hunter Blair's withering comment on the 'treasury of clichés' of those who saw the attack as driving a wedge between Briton and Briton.[29] He remarked further on how we cannot say whether the Northumbrians advanced from the north or from the east, and how Chester was eventually not in their territory, but that of Mercia.[30] Rachel Bromwich noted obscure allusions in the Welsh triads to supposed warriors at Chester, and the fame of Cynan Garwyn, including his campaigns against other Welshmen.[31] His unpopularity would be unremarkable. Sawyer summed up the conflict as fought for 'plunder and prestige, or the pursuit of old enmities'.[32] Dorothy Whitelock gave a useful version of Bede's text.[33]

In the 1980s, Archibald Duncan commented on sources for the battle, quoting the Irish allusion to Cetula, but without seeking to identify him.[34] In an edition of a seventh-century poem on Cynddylan of Powys, Geraint Gruffydd mentioned how David Dumville had cast a sceptical eye on the authenticity of the Cynan Garwyn poem, on the grounds that Powys did not exist in the sixth century.[35] Dumville repeated his doubts elsewhere.[36] Michael Wallace-Hadrill discussed sources of the battle, although not the Irish ones.[37] In the next decade Jenny Rowland spoke of the clash as directly between Bernicia and Powys. She discounted participation by Gwynedd, because Irish annals

---

[25] Alcock 1971, 136–38.
[26] Stenton 1971, 78.
[27] Williams 1972, 49, 84–85.
[28] Morris 1973, 238–39.
[29] Hunter Blair 1976, 41–42, 50.
[30] Hunter Blair 1977, 47.
[31] Bromwich 1978, 164, 318–19.
[32] Sawyer 1978, 25.
[33] Whitelock 1979, 662.
[34] Duncan 1981.
[35] Gruffydd 1982.
[36] Dumville 1988.
[37] Wallace-Hadrill 1988, 54, 218–19.

say nothing of it.[38] Despite that, Nick Higham goes against all opinion by seeing the Gwynedd ruler Iago as a victim of the battle.[39] More carefully, Ken Dark limits himself to noting Welsh and Irish annals for the death of Selyf at Chester, perhaps indicating it as a Powys city.[40] Nick Higham later used Iago's death in the year of the battle to portray him as the Church's protector of the Synod of Chester in 601.[41] Few will assent to this.

In the present century Thomas Charles-Edwards dates the battle to 613, following Irish annals which themselves probably derive from those in Iona. He refers to the killing of Selyf ap Cynan, regarded as ruling the polity developing out of the Romano-British civitas of the Cornovii (with Chester in their territory), which itself surely became the kingdom of Powys. He had no comment on Cetula.[42] Nick Higham thinks that an archaic elegy for Powys ruler Cynddylan, alluding to the 'book-clutching monks', echoes Bede on those of Bangor-is-Coed.[43] André Crépin repeated without a doubt the myth, discredited by Sir John Lloyd nearly a century ago, on how 'par leur victoire les Anglo-Saxons séparèrent définitivement les Gallois des autres Celtes brittaniques de Strathclyde'.[44] How difficult it is to destroy a facile untruth, even in Oxford. James Fraser dates the battle to 615.[45] James Campbell put the massacre of Bangor monks in the context of modern ethnic cleansing.[46] He was right on the brutality and wrong on the politics. The Northumbrians did not plan to settle at Bangor-is-Coed or Chester, and never did. They here contrast with Germans, Poles, Russians, Lithuanians, Ukrainians, Czechs, Slovaks, Hungarians, Serbs, Croats and others in central and eastern Europe, who in 1945 achieved national states with stable frontiers, but only (as Norman Davies remarked in his histories of Poland) after shedding oceans of blood. Tim Clarkson considers that the Northumbrians reached Chester through the Aire gap, in 615, and that they fought 'to extinguish a challenge to Æthelfrith's authority by a rival kingdom', probably that of Selyf, 'who perhaps saw an opportunity to extend his own infleunce across the Cheshire lowlands'.[47] Professor Sims-Williams doubts Dumville's scepticism on the derivation of Selyf from the Biblical 'Solomon'.[48]

---

[38] Rowland 1990, 126.
[39] Higham 1993, 88.
[40] Dark 1994, 109.
[41] Higham 1995, 131–32.
[42] Charles-Edwards 2001.
[43] Higham 2002, 178.
[44] Crépin and Lapidge 2005a, 296.
[45] Fraser 2009, 155.
[46] Campbell 2010.
[47] Clarkson 2010, 117.
[48] Sims-Williams 2011, 301n.92.

Most recently are two accounts which show the way that implications of the battle are still not dead. Professor Higham puts his finger on how Bede exploited the accounts of Gildas and the Chester campaign for political ends. Gildas had chastised the Britons, yet still thought of them as 'God's people in Britain'. Gildas was Bede's main source for late Roman Britain, but the role allocated to Britons could not be allowed to stand. God's chosen people there were now the English, the Britons being dismissed from divine protection. St Augustine had predicted that, if the Britons did not preach to the English, 'they would one day suffer the vengeance of death at their hands'; and Bede does not fail to add how 'this came to pass in every particular' at Chester. He regarded it as a just recompense to the Britons for their 'unspeakable crimes', 'inbred hatred' of the English, and 'evil customs'; fortunately, however, in Bede's day, the Welsh were 'opposed by the power of God and man alike' and were therefore politically impotent.[49] The modern equivalents of Bede's charged ideological interpretation of conquest and expropriation occur all over the world and need no underlining.

Just as Bede uses the discourse of imperialism, there is even now discourse from the other side, that of the dispossessed. Nearly 15 centuries after he wrote, Gildas still provides Welsh patriots with a morale-boosting theory of history, both in Church and State. We have already mentioned the original and stimulating ideas of A. W. Wade-Evans and Saunders Lewis on the Welsh as the sole nation in Britain with a history which comes directly from the Roman Empire and its official Christianity. It may be compared with the contrasting ideas of Gildas and Bede on the unity of Britain, a topic which can be traced from Roman times to today, when it is more debated than ever.[50] These persistent notions now provide background to Iestyn Daniel's translation of Gildas.[51] Some may find that what can be deduced from Gildas has an attraction and an interest, as the violent opinions (today repudiated by all) of Bede do not. So we can see how interpretations of the massacre at Chester given by Welsh historians of the seventeenth and eighteenth centuries have equivalents in the twenty-first, where readers of Dr Daniel's introduction will find echoes (no doubt unconscious) of Charles Maurras (1868–1952), French polemicist, right-wing theoretician, royalist, anti-Dreyfusard, and (in the eyes of some) patriot-martyr. One may note, too, how the comparable ideas on Church and State remain influential in Continental Europe and the United

---

[49] Higham 2018, 172–73.
[50] Rees 2000, 35–36.
[51] Daniel 2019, 123–24.

States (especially the South) in work on the Spanish philosopher J. F. Donoso Cortés (1809–1853).[52]

Such is the contribution of the Battle of Chester over hundreds of years to religious, cultural and nationalist debate. Let us add one more fact, on the identity of 'Cetula', the name, sounding more like that of a Roman matron than of a Welshman, does not look Welsh. It must be corrupt. Because transposition of letters is a common scribal error, especially here, given Latin nouns in -ula, we may emend to 'Cedual', a tolerable rendering of Cadwal or (in Old Welsh orthography) Cadgual. An otherwise unknown Cadwal gave his name to Kidwelly (= Cydweli), Carmarthenshire.[53] More relevant is Cadwal Crisban (= white shirt) in the Rhos genealogy cited above. His great-great-grandson Ceredig died in 798; his great-grandfather Cynlas was the object of Gildas's scorn in 536. A little thought suggests that a man active in 536 could have a great-grandson dying a hero's death in 613; a warrior killed in 613 could have an adult descendant dying five generations later in 798. On that basis, King Cadwal of Rhos seem to be the 'Cetula rex' who perished with Selyf at Chester in 613. It needs no imagination to see that a Northumbrian threat to Chester might concern a ruler of lowland Clwyd and Conway. We may add that Cadwal gained the epithet 'white shirt'. Whatever that means, he must have had renown. He was no petty king.

If our identification of 'Cetula' as Cadwal of Rhos is secure, it has several implications. With two Welsh kings dead in the fray, it is no surprise that the Battle of Chester should have been bloody. Bards in Rhos and Powys would have mourned the death of warriors from North and East. The conflict was a major one, with troops summoned from more than one part of Wales, and with two kings to command them; although the absence of Gwynedd, noted long ago by Sir John Lloyd, is also telling, not least in the light of aggression attributed to Selyf's father in the poem from the Taliesin corpus. However we understand them, we may perceive in our sources an antipathy between Gwynedd and Powys, which is of long duration. It reappears in texts of five centuries later, which mention Gwynedd, Dyfed, Glamorgan, Gwent and many other places of Wales, but Powys not once.[54] Finally, a comment on the original version of this paper, published in 2013. It closed with a comment on how, if emendation of 'Cetula' to Cedual (= Cadwal) could be accepted, one could look forward to more advances in knowledge 'once we relinquish a

---

[52] Kłos 2017.
[53] Owen and Morgan 2007, 206.
[54] Breeze 2009, 100–14.

superstitious trust in scribal infallibility'.[55] That prophecy can now be put to the test. Readers can judge for themselves what is said on Mount Badon and Arthur's battles, as well as other matters whereon I have challenged conventional thinking and belief persistence, in a volume appearing as this one went to press.[56]

[55] Breeze 2013.
[56] Evans and Fulton 2019.

Chapter 7

633: HATFIELD CHASE AND BRITISH VICTORY AT DONCASTER

The battle at Hatfield, usually taken as Hatfield Chase near Doncaster, is a historical might-have-been. It was at Hatfield in 633 that, in alliance with Penda of Mercia, Cadwallon of Gwynedd wiped out a Northumbria army under Edwin and for a year had the North at his mercy. Yet his defeat by Oswald near Hexham in late 634 destroyed for ever the dream of a Celtic *reconquista* in Britain. A dramatic turn of the tables has thus left *Haethfelth* as a footnote for historians, not a chapter heading. But it was no small engagement. Since there has been disagreement on where it was fought (Yorkshire or Powys?) and when, this paper sets out discussion of it between 1860 and 2013, beside showing what its Welsh name, *Meicen* or *Meigen*, tells us on events.

Early observers well understood the magnitude of Cadwallon's triumph. In its entry for 630, *Annales Cambriae* (using North British sources) states 'Battle of Meiceren (var. Meigen), and there Edwin was killed with his two sons. But Cadwallon was the victor.'[1] Plummer cited this (and *Historia Brittonum*, which names the sons as Osfrid and Eadfrid), giving the date as 633 and the place as Hatfield Chase, north-east of Doncaster.[2] He did not reflect that the combat was surely south-east of the town, at the chase's southern edge, on the Roman road from Lincoln. He also quoted the Annals of Tigernach and Annals of Ulster on the event, which mention Edwin, Cadwallon and Penda, but not where they fought. On the aftermath of battle (dated to 633) Anderson quoted a Latin life of St Oswald by Reginald of Durham (active 1162–73), with the statement on how Anfrid returned from Scottish exile to rule Bernicia for a year (while Edwin's son Osui took over Deira).[3]

Full and careful information was given by Sir John Lloyd (1861–1947), as expected. He observed that the 'scene of this memorable encounter cannot, unfortunately, be fixed with certainty'. Bede implies somewhere in Deira or

---

[1] Williams 1860, 7.
[2] Plummer 1896, II, 115–16.
[3] Anderson 1908, 13.

bordering it, but the Welsh called the spot *Meicen*, later identified with Meigen, near Breiddin Hill, north-east of Welshpool, Powys. Sensing confusion of two places with the same name, Lloyd opted for the northern location as site of the battle.[4] On *Annales Cambriae* and other chronicles, the Chadwicks stressed their northern or Strathclyde sources, including the entries on Cadwallon's two battles, which they dated to 633 and 634.[5] A summary history notices how, according to Reginald of Durham's life of Oswald, Cadwallon had before the campaign forced Penda into submission and married his sister.[6] Geoffrey of Monmouth mentioned the battle, adding (bogusly) that the King of Orkney was one of the dead: his translator, unaware of Old Welsh *Meicen*, called it 'Hedfelt'.[7] Levison dated the conflict and Edwin's death to 12 October 633.[8]

The Powys candidate appears in the comment that 'Mrs Bromwich [1915–2010] informs me that she has reason to suspect that the equation of *Meicen* with *Haethfelth* is incorrect'.[9] Kenneth Jackson (1909–1991) was more informative. Analysing the ninth-century *Historia Brittonum*, he took *Haethfelth* as Hatfield Chase, near Doncaster, and the date as 632. As the *Meigen* where Cadwallon allegedly fought was in Powys, he thought that a Welsh victory near the Don had been confused with a previous one on the Welsh border.[10] Sir Idris Foster was more obscure. Penda's alliance with Cadwallon brought about the death of Edwin in 632 at Hatfield Chase 'according to Bede: or *in bello Meicen* as Nennius tells us (later Welsh tradition places *gueith Meicen* near the boundaries of Powys)'.[11] With typical unhelpfulness, Sir Idris left readers to work out that *gueith* is Old Welsh for 'battle'. They could not work out at all from his words whether the conflict really was in Powys (despite the implications in Bede) or whether this is an error of bardic commentators.

The Ordnance Survey (OS) Map for the period is forthright. It puts *Haethfelth* south-east of Doncaster between the rivers Don and Torne.[12] A possible place for the engagement would be where the Roman road from Lincoln, the main northern route to York which did not cross the Humber, went over the Torne by Rossington Bridge (National Grid Reference (NGR) SK 6299). Toponyms in *carr* around the spot south of the modern Hatfield Moors (NGR

[4] Lloyd 1911, 186.
[5] Chadwick and Chadwick 1932, 144, 148.
[6] Williams 1941, 78–79.
[7] Lewis 1942, 279.
[8] Levison 1946, 272.
[9] Hunter Blair 1954, 137–72.
[10] Jackson 1963, 20–62.
[11] Foster 1965, 213–35.
[12] *Map of Britain in the Dark Ages.*

SE 6905) are relics of its ancient marshes. Yet *Meicen* does not figure on the OS map, unlike other Welsh forms for English places. Kenneth Jackson, adviser on such terms, must have considered identification of *Haethfelth* with *Meicen* as risky. Kirby puts Edwin's violent death in 634, but with no clue where.[13] The standard edition of Bede's history shows no doubts on Hatfield Chase or the date (12 October 633).[14]

In this context Jackson referred to an obscure bardic praise-poem on Cadwallon, which speaks of 'the muster for the burning of York'. Jackson took this as alluding to Cadwallon's devastation of Northumbria after Hatfield Chase in 633.[15] It did not occur to him that, if so, the poet's silence on *Meicen* is strange. The lines were surely composed before the campaign, not after. Hunt Blair dated the battle to 12 October 632, but with no comment on its whereabouts.[16] Alcock observed that the confusion between the Yorkshire site (30 miles from Edwin's capital at York and only 65 miles from Penda's at Tamworth) and the one in Powys 'has not been resolved', although it might be due to conflation of two events in the Easter annals. Having it both ways, he spoke therefore of an initial conflict on the Welsh frontier followed by a 'shattering victory' on the road to York.[17] Stenton remarked that the armies met 'at an unknown spot in the region now called Hatfield Chase' on 12 October 632.[18] Mayr-Harting nevertheless gave the date as 633.[19]

A curious view was expressed by Glanville Jones of Leeds. He cited a medieval Welsh triad which 'reveals Cefn Digoll (the Long Mountain) in the Chirbury district as the scene of a victory won in the early seventh century by the Welsh, under the leadership of Cadwallon of Gwynedd, over the English, led by Edwin of Northumbria'.[20] More compelling are words of Sir Ifor Williams (1881–1965). He recognized Cadwallon's 'thirst for vengeance', with the joint Welsh-Mercian assault on the North being 'a scheme on the grand scale', and quoted Stenton's verdict on Cadwallon as 'the only British king of historic times who overthrew an English dynasty'. He then summarized the eulogy on Cadwallon, obviously written before the invasion. As it lauds its subject to the skies, Williams wondered how the bard improved on it 'when news came later of resounding victories in the North'. He quoted Bede on how, after the defeat, Edwin's head was taken away to avoid dishonour and was buried

---

[13] Kirby 1967, 57.
[14] Colgrave and Mynors 1969, 203.
[15] Jackson 1969, 61.
[16] Hunter Blair 1970, 97.
[17] Alcock 1971, 139, 338.
[18] Stenton 1971, 80–81, 116.
[19] Mayr-Harting 1972, 68.
[20] Jones 1972, 279–382.

eventually in what is now York Minster.[21] It had to be. Northumbrian morale would have suffered to see it brandished on a pole by jubilant Welshmen. In a similar spirit, Northumbrian troops were to rescue the head and hands of Oswald, nailed up by Penda after the battle of *Maserfelth* (near Forden, Powys) in 642.

On a more rhetorical level, Morris told of Cadwallon's triumph, when for a year he 'ruled as a high king from the Thames to the Forth, supreme over British and English underkings. Had his rule endured he might have recovered London and the South, and restored the empire of Arthur.' One night dispelled those ambitions, when his empire 'quickly collapsed', destroyed in a single battle.[22] Morris was trained as an ancient historian and the ghosts of Plutarch and Tacitus gesture in his account of hubris followed by dramatic peripetia. Duncan accepted Kirby's revised chronology with Edwin's catastrophic defeat in 634.[23] (It is implicit as well in the date 635 for Oswald's killing of Cadwallon.) Hunter Blair still gave the day of *Haethfelth* as 12 October 632. He drew attention to a curious episode in the life of St Gregory (the work of an unknown Whitby nun), concerning a priest instructed in a dream to seek Edwin's bones. He dithered, but (after the figure in his dream threatened him and flogged him with a whip) did as he was told. Bones were eventually found and buried in the state at Whitby, that royal mausoleum. Spirits of those who died in battle were later seen at *Haethfelth*, visiting their bodies and confounding sceptics. No mention is made of Edwin's head at York (Bede's view).[24]

Hunter Blair had an acute comment elsewhere. He observed that two of the major clashes between northern and southern English, by the Idle in 616 and Hatfield in 633, occurred on the Roman road from Lincoln to York via Doncaster.[25] It places the battle south-east of Doncaster, not by Hatfield to the north-east. He might have added a third conflict, that of Penda's crushing defeat by Oswiu on the *Uinued* in November 655. The OS Map mentioned above locates this where the Roman road from York crosses the River Went, 11 miles north-west of Doncaster.[26] No sane commander would take his forces on the alternative route from Lincoln to York via a ferry over the Humber. Logistical problems aside, it presented a death trap for his troops. Maps thus imply a battlefield south-east of Doncaster, perhaps on the River Torne, with Edwin's men trying to block a Welsh-Mercian advance on Doncaster. Once

[21] Williams 1972, 85–86, 143n.61.
[22] Morris 1973, 240.
[23] Duncan 1974, 60–61.
[24] Finberg 1974, 26–27.
[25] Hunter Blair 1976, 44, 130.
[26] Hunter Blair 1977, 255.

the defence was routed, the road to York was open and the capital left helpless against attack and plunder.

A later and semi-legendary poem on Cadwallon's campaigns, which is not the archaic seventh-century eulogy already referred to, has been edited (in Welsh). It contains mention of his triumph at Meigen, which he 'set ablaze', but the context shows this to be near Welshpool, Powys.[27] It was not in Yorkshire. The late triad is also edited (in English), with a long note on *Meigen*. The place in the triad is evidently Meigen in Powys, the region east of Welshpool around the Long Mountain (NGR SJ 2606), a massif separating England from Wales. On etymology, Dr Bromwich related *Meigen* to the personal name *Maig*.[28] We shall return to this.

Professor Sawyer, commenting briefly on the action at Hatfield Chase in 633, also described Lindsey (north Lincolnshire) as Mercian territory and the Trent from an early date as the boundary between Mercia and Northumbria.[29] Hence the succession of battles on the western route from Lincoln to York, where the south-eastern approach to Doncaster had a vital strategic importance as a corridor between marshlands. That *Haethfelth* and Hatfield Chase were one and the same place is confirmed by the Whitby life's anecdote of a southern priest called Trimma, told in a dream to look for Edwin's bones. They were 'in the district which is called Hatfield', and he was helped to find them by a certain Teoful in Lindsey. Trima later dwelt near the battlefield, often saw spirits of four dead warriors returning in splendour to their bodies and expressed a wish to build a monastery there.[30] That a man from near Lincoln aided him proves that *Haethfelth* was nowhere near Wales. It was surely between Lincoln and Doncaster. Trimma's ghost story may even confirm that. A study rationalist might regard his 'spirits' as marsh gas, catching fire when mixed with phosphuretted hydrogen. Hence, perhaps, their 'splendour'.

As regards dating there has been a return to Bede's 633, despite arguments for 632 or 634. On *Meigen* in Wales, it is suggested that the Welsh chronicles 'confused an earlier victory over Edwin with the northern battle of Hatfield Chase'.[31] Hatfield Chase is elsewhere related to the concept of British *imperium*. Here too is the statement *tout court* that Edwin 'fought at Meigen, near modern Welshpool'.[32] Early Welsh presentations of Cadwallon as triumphant hero (but without mention of Penda) have also been set out.[33]

---

[27] Gruffydd 1978, 25–43.
[28] Bromwich 1978b, 152–53.
[29] Sawyer 1978, 29, 38.
[30] Whitelock 1979, 750–51.
[31] Rowland 1990, 129.
[32] Stancliffe 1995, 84–96.
[33] Higham 2002, 158.

The etymology of *Haethfelth* as 'heath-covered open land' now has definitive expression.[34] An account of Cadwallon brings together much useful information, but has nothing of his defeat of Edwin.[35] A further one, including some mistranslations of early Welsh, identifies him as another British ruler, but with comment on our battle.[36] Its proposal on two Cadwallons has been doubted. Most recently, we hear of an attack by Edwin 'in Meigen' (around Welshpool), with the Welsh giving as good as they got, particularly Cadwallon, 'leader of the alliance responsible for slaying Edwin, the first Christian king of Northumbria'.[37] It shows how the notion of a Northumbrian attack on the border of Powys persists, despite evidence in the Whitby life of St Gregory.

As soon as this paper's original version was written, three descriptions of the battle came to hand. Thomas Charles-Edwards attributes Edwin's death to 'a rebellion led by Cadwallon, king of the Britons, with the aid of Penda, of the Mercian royal kindred' in late 633. It is contrasted with *Maserfelth* in 642. In the first, Cadwallon and Penda challenged a Deiran overlord on Deira's frontier. In the second, Oswald (a Bernician) led an army to the border of Mercia and Wales. By now (according to Bede), leadership of the anti-Northumbrian alliance had passed to Penda.[38]

The two other references may be dealt with briefly. Marged Haycock thinks that 'Meigen need not be in or near Powys at all'. Citing a suggestion of 1936 by the learned but eccentric scholar Egerton Phillimore (1856–1937), she locates the battlefield as perhaps on the River Meden, Derbyshire.[39] We give this short shrift. Phillimore will not have known the statements in the anonymous life of St Gregory, which makes the location near Doncaster certain. The information offered was retrograde even in 1936. As for Timothy Venning, he gives Edwin's defeat as being 'near Doncaster on 12 October 633 (or possibly 634), indicating a Mercian-Gwynedd advance on his southern frontier'.[40] No mention of Powys, one notes, if lingering uncertainly on the date.

Let us now try to clarify the issues by analysis of Old Welsh *Meicen* (later *Meigen*). Its derivation from the personal form *Maig* is tucked away in a study of Welsh river names, which refers to various Welshman called *Maig*, and to *Meigion* 'district of Maig' as an old name for the area around Bridgnorth, Shropshire.[41] If there was a *Meigion* in east Shropshire, Meigen by Welshpool

[34] Watts 2004, 286.
[35] Woolf 2004, 5–24.
[36] Fraser 2009, 166–68.
[37] Stancliffe 2010, 68–83.
[38] Charles-Edwards 2013, 345, 390, 393.
[39] Haycock 2013, 7–39.
[40] Venning 2013, 52.
[41] Thomas 1938, 103.

need not be unique. We may hence turn the clock back to 1911, when Sir John Lloyd proposed that a place so called near Doncaster was confused with one in Powys. Once the Celtic names for regions conquered by the English were forgotten, such an error was natural. That appears to make sense of the evidence. Because the suggestion that Edwin was defeated by Cadwallon on the upper Severn is feeble, we rule it out. There was one great victory of Cadwallon over the Northumbrians, and it was on the approaches to the Don.

So we may look at maps of early medieval Britain with new confidence. We can feel sure that *Haethfelth*, on the inland route from Lincoln to the North, was known in Old Welsh as *Meicen* (giving modern Welsh *Meigen*). It has parallels. Oswiu's defeat of Penda in 655 on the *Uinued* or Went was known to the Welsh as the battle of *Gaii campus* (field of Gaius), commemorating an otherwise forgotten Romano-Briton. *Meicen* resembles that as a survival from the early British past. It is not a translation of an English form or pseudo-learned invention. As such it differs from Old Welsh *din guairoi* (stadium fort) or Bamburgh and *Cantscaul* (warrior's enclosure) or Hexham in *Historia Brittonum*, or Bishop Asser's *Tigguocobauc* (cavy house) for Nottingham.[42] Another instance is *Rhydychen* for 'Oxford' in the twelfth-century *Four Branches of the Mabinogi*, which translates the English name (not vice versa).[43] The four Welsh toponyms all postdate the corresponding English ones. *Meicen* will do the opposite. It predates the English settlements, not vice versa.

The above was published in 2014.[44] Nothing appearing since seems to have changed its conclusions, although one may add a reference on why the anonymous Whitby life of St Gregory is attributed to a nun, and not to a monk.[45] There will also now be an account of poems on Cadwallon in a Cambridge history coming out as this book went to press.[46] Even so, what is said there is unlikely to modify the upshot of the above. Edwin and his army met their doom on 12 October 633, the date given by Bede, who was in a position to know the facts. This dramatic event took place south-east of Doncaster on the old road from Lincoln, where it fringes the marshland of *Haethfelth*, later Hatfield chase. There is no reason to think that Edwin previously met Cadwallon in combat and was worsted at Meigen in north-east Powys, the evidence for that consisting of late traditions in a triad and a legendary poem. We agree with Sir John Lloyd (1911) that the Welsh name of *Haethfelth* became forgotten, and so the action was transferred to the sole Meigen that the Welsh then knew, near Welshpool.

---

[42] Koch 2007, map 23.
[43] Breeze 2009, 28–29.
[44] Breeze 2014.
[45] Breeze 2012b.
[46] Evans and Fulton 2019.

Chapter 8

634: *HEFENFELD* AND BRITISH DEFEAT IN NORTHUMBERLAND

After ravaging Northumbria for over a year, Cadwallon of Gwynedd was killed in the winter of 634–35, when his army was surprised and routed by Oswald of Bernicia at *Denisesburn*, now Rowley Burn (National Grid Reference (NGR) NY 9358), three miles south of Hexham, Northumberland. This chapter deals with the circumstances of the battle and specifically with *Hefenfeld*. It was there, on the north side of Hexham, that Oswald and his men camped before attack, with Oswald raising a cross at the spot and praying for victory. Bede here tells us much, as noted by Dr Catherine Clarke. Discussing his account of *Dryhthelm*, she says,

> Dryhthelm is denied entry into these paradisal landscapes until after death, but the *Ecclesiastical History* continually hints at the possibility of realizing the heavenly on earth and, more importantly, on English soil. When Oswald's Christian Saxon army defeats the British pagans at Heavenfield in 642, Bede notes the name of the place in both Latin and English. 'This place is called in English Heavenfield, and in Latin *Caelestis Campus*, a name which it certainly received in days of old as an omen of future happenings' (*Vocantur locus ille lingua Anglorum Hefenfeld, quod dici potest latine 'Caelestis campus', quod certo utique praesagio futurorum antiquitus nomen accepit*). The place of battle and suffering is transformed into an image of heaven, recalling both the paradisial claims of Dryhthelm's vision and the Edenic image of *Britannia* which opens the *History*. Clearly, the narratives of specific individuals and places can be seen as microcosmic performances of the myth central to the *Ecclesiastical History*: the aspiration to re-discover and recover an ideal, unfallen state through faith and struggle.[1]

---

[1] Clarke 2006, 26.

Whatever one thinks of her interpretation, Professor Clarke was cavalier with the facts. Oswald's army was Anglian, not Saxon; its Welsh enemies were Christians, not pagans; the battle was fought not at Heavenfield, but several miles away; and it took place in the winter of 634–35, not 642. Her 'vocantur' is a mistake for Bede's *vocatur*. Battles and Latin grammar are not the strong point of Catherine Clarke, or (it seems) of Southampton University, where she now has a Chair of English.

However, reference to better historians also reveals inconsistency and error, as we shall see. The Tudor antiquary Leland reported on the matter thus. 'There is a fame that Oswald won the batelle at Halydene, a two miles est from St Oswalde's asche.'[2] Further details occur in a later edition. 'And that Haliden is it that Bede callith Hevenfeld. And the men theraboute yet finde smaule wod crossis in the grounde.'[3] *Halydene* (holy valley) has been taken as the old name of Hallington (NGR NY 9875), two miles east of the Roman road from Corbridge to Lothian, and four miles north of the Wall. Despite this, other writers locate Oswald's camp far closer to the Roman Wall and deny that it was the actual place of battle.

Sir John Lloyd thus noted how Oswald set up a rough wooden cross at his camp, and knelt with his warriors at its foot to pray for victory. 'The spot bore the name of Heavenfield; it lay close to the Roman Wall, not far from the point where this is cut by the North Tyne, and the devotion of later ages, which held the place to be one of the most sacred in Northumbria, raised there the chapel of St Oswald's, which marks it to this day.' Advancing to the south by night, Oswald's hosts made a dawn attack on Cadwallon at Rowley Burn, slew him and routed his much greater forces. With a great historian's scrupulous regard for facts, Lloyd was careful to point out that Bede nowhere suggests that battle was actually fought at Heavenfield.[4] Bede states that Cadwallon was overwhelmed at *Denisesburn*, the modern Rowley Burn. This accords with Adomnán's statements in his life of St Columba that Oswald's army was small, but won an easy victory by a night's march and surprise assault at daybreak. Thanks to Lloyd, Celticists have tended to accuracy on this point, unlike others. Williams hence declared that Oswald defeated Cadwallon's army near Heavenfield in 634, adding that this figures as *bellum Cantscaul* in the ninth-century *Historia Brittonum*.[5] Despite this, Hunter Blair referred to Cadwallon's death at *Hefenfelth* in 634.[6] Jackson,

---

[2] Plummer 1896, II, 123.
[3] Smith 1910, 61.
[4] Lloyd 1911, 187–88.
[5] Williams 1941, 79.
[6] Hunter Blair 1954, 163.

correctly locating Oswald's defeat of Cadwallon at Rowley Burn, explained *Cantscaul* in *Annales Cambriae* and *Historia Brittonum*, citing a paper of 1933 by Sir Ifor Williams. It is the Old Welsh for 'enclosure of a young warrior', equivalent to Old English *Hagustaldesham* (village of a young warrior) or Hexham. The Welsh were addicted to such toponymic calques (as with *Rhydychen* (ford of oxen = Oxford)), although their translation is not quite correct here, since they apparently took *ham* (with long *a*) (village) as Old English *hamm* (enclosure).[7]

The OS Map for the period includes *Hefenfelth* (as it gives it), located well to the south-west of Hallington, immediately north of the Roman Wall and east of the North Tyne. It is shown with the crossed swords of a battlefield, which is misleading.[8] Needham gave a useful note here. Commenting on *seo stow is gehaten Heofonfeld on Englisc* in Ælfric's *Lives of the Saints* (completed by 1002), he referred to the link with Hallington reported by Leland, but he said further that the chapel of St Oswald-in-Lee, built about 1737, stands just north of the Roman Wall some five miles south-west of Hallington and four miles north of Hexham. It is marked on the Ordnance Survey Map (NGR NY 936696).[9] Lloyd's comment notwithstanding, Kirby referred to Cadwallon's death at the Battle of Heavenfield near Hexham, and dated it to 635.[10]

Colgrave and Mynors gave the form as *Hefenfeld* and translated Bede on it as follows, with his belief on how the name

> signified that a heavenly sign was to be erected there, a heavenly victory won and that heavenly miracles were to take place there, continuing to this day. The place, on its north side, is close to the wall with which the Romans once girded the whole of Britain from sea to sea, to keep off the attacks of the barbarians as already described. To this place the brethren of the church of Hexham, not far away, have long made it their custom to come every year, on the day before that [5 August] on which King Oswald was killed, to keep vigil there for the benefit of his soul, to sing many psalms of praise, and, next morning, to offer up the holy sacrifice and oblation on his behalf. And since that good custom has spread, a church has lately been built there, so that the place has become still more sacred and worthy of honour in the eyes of all.[11]

[7] Jackson 1963b, 34, 45.
[8] *Map of Britain in the Dark Ages.*
[9] Needham 1966, 29.
[10] Kirby 1967, 58.
[11] Colgrave and Mynors 1969, 216–17.

A comment on the significance of the form was given by Hunter Blair. He located the battle at 'a site which came to be called Heavenfield, doubtless because of its association with a victory won by a king whose posthumous fame as saint and martyr' was widespread.[12] His 'came to be' cannot, alas, be correct. It contrasts with the precision of Alcock. Having referred to Cadwallon's death at Rowley Burn, he said this: 'The battle is usually referred to "Heavenfield", but this name rightly belongs to the place where Oswald set up a wooden cross and sought for divine aid, probably on the night before the action, which began with a dawn attack.'[13] Stenton, who was silent on Heavenfield, dated Oswald's victory to the last weeks of 633.[14] Heavenfield also figures in Professor Thomas's discussion of early relics, as follows: 'A wooden cross, which Oswald had set up with his own hands at Heavenfield, on the Wall, in 633 to commemorate his victory, was also regarded as sacred; the drinking of water in which splinters from this cross had been soaked cured both men and beasts.'[15] But Oswald raised the cross before the battle, not after. How could he commemorate a victory which he had not won?

In a last comment on the conflict, Hunter Blair said, 'Cadwallon himself was killed near Hexham in 634 after his defeat by Oswald in the battle' near the Roman Wall.[16] This implies two combats, not one; as if Oswald worsted Cadwallon by the Wall to finish him off later, although this is not what Bede and Adomnán say. So much was made clear by Whitelock. She conveniently provided in one volume the statements on the campaign given by *Historia Brittonum*, Bede and Adomnán. The first tells how Oswald 'killed Cadwallon, king of the district of Gwynedd, in the battle of *Cantscaul*, with a great slaughter' of his army. Bede's comment she gave thus: 'That place is called in the English language "Heavenfield", which can be rendered *caelestis campus* in Latin, which name it obviously received of old as a presage of future events, denoting, surely, that the heavenly trophy was to be erected there, a heavenly victory begun, and heavenly miracles performed until today.' Finally, Adomnán describes the dream that Oswald had before the battle, when St Columba assured him of success. 'The ensuing night, just as he had been instructed in the vision, King Oswald advanced from the camp to battle against many thousands with a much smaller army, and, as had been promised him, he was granted by the Lord a happy and easy victory.' Adomnán adds that his information came from his predecessor Failbhe, abbot of Iona in 669–79, who

---

[12] Hunter Blair 1970, 101–102.

[13] Alcock 1971, 140.

[14] Stenton 1971, 81.

[15] Thomas 1971, 133.

[16] Hunter Blair 1977, 51.

heard it from Seghine, abbot of Iona in 623–52, who was told it by Oswald himself.[17]

Discussing the divine power which Christianity offered to Anglo-Saxon rulers, Campbell cited the cross raised by Oswald before the battle that made him king. 'In that sign he conquered. They called the site of the battle and of the cross Heavenfield.'[18] Once again, a historian takes Heavenfield as the battlefield and maintains that it was called after the victory. Two errors. Better is a remark of Wallace-Hadrill.[19] 'Bede supposes that the place-name *Hefenfeld* was older than the battle that took place there: in other words, that the name foretold the event.'[20]

Higham dates Oswald's victory to either 634 or 635, despite Stenton's reference to the last weeks of 633.[21] Another volume on Oswald has a lengthy account of his death in battle in 642 (mistakenly put at Oswestry, and not near Forden, Powys).[22] Charles-Edwards alludes merely to how Cadwallon 'unexpectedly fell in battle against Oswald'.[23] Thereafter, Crépin offered welcome scepticism, noting that *Hefenfeld* is '*Heofen-feld* dans la version vieil-anglaise, qui ne croit pas nécessaire d'expliquer le composé *heaven-field*', and then quotes the somewhat misleading passage by Leland on Hallington.

That concludes the first part of this paper. It allows six conclusions. First, the Old English form is *Hefenfeld*, not *Hefenfelth*; second, this place was the site of Oswald's camp, but not his defeat of Cadwallon; third, that the campaign was in the November or December of 634; fourth, that Heavenfield lay just north of the Wall and east of the North Tyne, being some miles from modern Hallington, on which matter Leland's account is valuable but confusing; fifth, that the toponym existed before the campaign and was not the result of victory; sixth, that the cross was raised before battle, and not afterwards. Perhaps more significant here, however, is the respect one gains for the accuracy and precision of scholars like Lloyd, Stenton, Alcock and Wallace-Hadrill, as opposed to the errors found in others.

The last part of this paper contains a proposal for a new derivation for *Hefenfeld* (where *feld* is Old English for 'open land', and does not mean 'field' in the modern sense) or *Caelestis Campus*. Bede thought that the name existed before the battle and was prophetic. How, then, did so unusual a toponym

---

[17] Whitelock 1979, 263, 678, 752.
[18] Campbell 1982b, 56.
[19] Wallace-Hadrill 1988, 89.
[20] Higham 1995, 138.
[21] Stancliffe 1995, 84–96.
[22] Charles-Edwards 2001, 92.
[23] Crépin and Lapidge 2005b, 20.

come into existence, since 'heaven' is so unlikely to be a place-name element in any language? At first sight one might explain the form from the Old English personal name *Hefa*, as with Hevingham in Norfolk, understood as 'homestead of followers of (a man called) Hefa'. Against this is the spelling *Hefenfeld* with *e*, when the genitive singular of *Hefa* would be *Hefan* 'Hefa's'.[24] Another explanation, however, seems more likely.

Now, Bede's *Caelestis campus* is a curious expression. In the *Ecclesiastical History* it is paralleled by a reference to Durrow (Co. Laois) as *campus roborum* (plain of oaks), while an annal for 750 in the Moore Bede mentions *campus Cyil*, the plain of Kyle around Ayr, Scotland.[25] These have equivalents in Welsh-Latin writing. The battlefield of the *Uinued* in November 655, when Northumbrian forces crushed the Mercians, is given as *campus Gaii* (plain of Gaius) in *Annales Cambriae* and *Historia Brittonum*.[26] There are other Welsh-Latin parallels. A life of St Padarn refers to part of Brittany as *campus Heli* (compare Welsh *heli*, 'brine, salt water').[27] A charter related to St Dyfrig mentions *campus Malochu* (where *Malochu* is a personal name), identified with Mawfield Farm (NGR SO 4436), west of Hereford; while *Historia Brittonum* tells how Vortigern's messengers found Ambrosius Aurelianus playing with a friend on *campus Elleti*, somewhere by the River Thaw in Glamorgan.[28]

Since Welsh-Latin used *campus Gaii* (plain of Gaius) for the battlefield of the *Uinued*, where the Roman road from York to Doncaster crosses the River Went, *Caelestis campus* may be explained not as 'heavenly plain' but 'plain of Caelestis'. It would be a similar place-name survival from Roman times. There is no difficulty about *Caelestis* as a personal name in Celtic Britain. A fifth-century inscription at Barmouth in south Gwynedd reads CAELEXTI MONEDORIGI, '(monument of) Caelestis Monedorix ("mountain king")'.[29] The evidence suggests that, just as the point where the York–Doncaster highway crossed the Went was known in British-Latin tradition as *campus Gaii*, so the defensive site used by Oswald was known as *Caelestis campus*, presumably after a local British chieftain or lord, a namesake of the fifth-century Caelestis of North Wales. Northumbrian settlers, failing to recognize the personal name in the genitive case here, and taking *Caelestis* as a masculine adjective, seemingly translated the toponym as *Hefenfeld*. Thereafter Bede could exercise sacred wit on the form, even though in origin it had no more to do with the

---

[24] Campbell 1959, 248.
[25] Colgrave and Mynors 1969, 222, 574.
[26] Whitelock 1979, 263.
[27] Wade-Evans 1944, 260.
[28] Doble 1971, 73, 149.
[29] Williams 1972, 9.

Christian heaven than, say, *Angli* (Angles) in an anonymous Whitby nun's life of St Gregory had to do with *angeli*, or *Deire* ('valiant ones', as with Welsh *dewr* 'brave') to do with *de ira Dei*.[30]

This explanation apparently makes sense of the puzzling form *Hefenfeld* (heaven plain). It will be a faulty translation of British-Latin *Caelestis campus* (plain of Caelestis). Like the *campus Gaii* of Welsh historical tradition, it was a site of military significance (unsurprisingly, given its closeness to the Roman Wall). As a toponym deriving from a Roman personal name it has a nearby equivalent in *Habitancum*, the fort (eight miles north-west of Hallington) at Risingham (NGR NY 8986), which was called after Habitus or Avitus, presumably a Romanized Briton who originally owned the site.[31] If, then, British-Latin *Caelestis campus* (plain of Caelestis) underlies *Hefenfeld*, this explanation provides a new glimpse of Britain's pre-English toponymy (as preserved by Bede), and of Anglo-Saxon encounters with the Latin spoken in the region of Hadrian's Wall.

Postscript: The above reproduces and develops a paper appearing in 2007.[32] To later sources already cited may be added one more, with scattered references to the Barmouth standing stone and the CAELEXTI MONEDORIGI inscribed upon it.[33] Nothing is said, however, on Bede's *Caelestis campus* as further evidence for the currency of this form in early Britain.

[30] Whitelock 1979, 747.
[31] Rivet and Smith 1979, 293, 371–72.
[32] Breeze 2007.
[33] Edwards 2013.

Chapter 9

642: *MASERFELTH* AND KING OSWALD'S DEATH AT FORDEN, POWYS

Maserfelth was where Penda of Mercia in 642 defeated Oswald of Northumbria, who was killed in the battle. It was a dramatic event, emphasized by Bede, who describes miracles later occurring at the spot, which he took as that of a martyrdom. Despite these clues, its location has been obscure. Yet the traditional identification with Oswestry (National Grid Reference (NGR) SJ 2929) in Shropshire was rightly rejected by the place-name scholar Margaret Gelling. A better answer can now be given on the basis of a communication to Ferdinand Holthausen by Max Förster (1869–1954) of Munich, who derived *Maser-* from Welsh. *Maser-*, relating to place names near Welshpool, Powys, thus apparently denotes the *-felth* or plain of the Severn close to Forden, where a Roman road enters Wales. As for the battle's Old Welsh name *Cocboy* (where *coc-* perhaps denotes a hillock), this seems to be Castle Mound (NGR SJ 2301), a conspicuous outcrop in Forden parish.

Now for the details. The Battle of *Maserfelth*, where the pagan king Penda killed Oswald of Northumbria, has been at once famous and obscure. Thanks to Bede, it has never been forgotten; but why it was fought and what happened on the field of conflict remain obscure. Its importance was still recognized by Britons and Saxons alike. Even though nothing shows that the Welsh took part in the engagement (a struggle for mastery among the English), *Annales Cambriae* has an entry for 644, 'Battle of *Cocboy*, in which fell Oswald king of the Northumbrians and Eoba king of the Mercians'.[1] Difficulties begin when we try to locate it. Plummer had notes on Bede's account of the battle, and referred to late traditions of it at Oswestry, near Offa's Dyke.[2] At the same time *Maserfelth* was explained tentatively as 'open space of maple trees', despite phonological difficulties for *maser* (which, if signifying 'maple', should not

---

[1] Williams ab Ithel 1860, 7.
[2] Plummer 1896, II, 152–53.

have *a* as first vowel) and absence of the element from other English toponyms, where the word for this tree is *mapuldor*.[3]

On the location at Oswestry, Sir John Lloyd regarded Old Welsh *Cocboy* as counting neither for nor against it. But he saw 'much in favour' of accepting *Maserfelth* as Oswestry, because 'Bede's account of the miracles which signalized the spot' implies somewhere 'in a wild region sometimes visited by British wayfarers'.[4] An advance was made when Sir Ifor Williams drew attention to *Cogwy* (from Old Welsh *Cocboy*) in Middle Welsh poetry.[5] In a eulogy of St Tysilio, active in the seventh century at Meifod in Montgomeryshire, Powys, the twelfth-century bard Cynddelw mentioned the battle of *Cogwy*, Oswald, and his brother Oswy.[6] Tysilio himself had no part in the events of 642. Yet the place name *Cogwy* is real enough. While twentieth-century Welshmen were discussing *Cogwy*, Germans were discussing *Maserfelth*, with Max Förster of Munich rejecting the sense 'open land of maples' and proposing 'Meisir's open land, Meisir's field'. Tucked away in the *Nachlese* of a dictionary, it refers to no published source.[7] Presumably it was a personal communication of Förster. His suggestion is fundamental and has been virtually unnoticed in Britain.

Meisir is a rare Welsh female name. But there was a Powys princess called Meisir, perhaps the lady of *Bryn-cae-meisir* (NGR SJ 1100) (hill by Meisir's field) nine miles south-west of Welshpool. Cynddelw was not the only bard to know of *Cogwy*. A stanza in an anonymous cycle spoken by Heledd, princess of Powys and sister to Meisir, refers to the 'field of *Cogwy*' in the context of warriors and her heroic brother Cynddylan. The verse implies that Powys was fatally involved in the battle, although there is no historical evidence for that. Heledd speaks as well of *Diffrynt Meissir* (Meisir's Vale). Despite references in medieval records to *Llys Veissir* (Meisir's court), the Welsh name of Maesbury south of Oswestry, Sir Ifor Williams (in setting out all this information) took the verses as indicating a valley by Bryn-cae-meisir, not far from Welshpool.[8] The implication is clear. *Maserfelth*, also known as *Cogwy*, was in or near Powys.

The battle of 'Maserfield', which 'may have been near Oswestry', figures in a summary history.[9] It appears too in Geoffrey of Monmouth's *Historia* under the name 'Brune' or 'Burne' (giving *Burnei* in the Welsh translation, which knows nothing of *Cogwy*). Geoffrey's form seems adapted from *Denisesburna*,

---

[3] Toller 1898, 661, 671.
[4] Lloyd 1911, 188–89.
[5] Williams 1926–28, 59–62.
[6] Lewis 1931, 180.
[7] Holthausen 1932–34, 428.
[8] Williams 1935, 209.
[9] Williams 1941, 79.

near Hexham, where Oswald killed Cadwallon in 634.[10] It will be one of his cavalier treatments of place names, like identifying Arthur's Mount Badon as Bath, or relocating the Battle of Camlan in Cornwall, or applying the name of Caradoc (near Ross-on-Wye) to Salisbury. 'Maserfield' appears (with a query) at Oswestry in a standard atlas.[11] Hunter Blair thought that, if Penda and Oswald met near Oswestry, the Welsh were surely involved, because of the *Annales Cambriae* entry, although Bede and early Welsh sources make no reference to it.[12] This goes beyond the evidence. Yet one needs little imagination to see that Mercian annihilation of a Northumbrian army had implications for Powys and beyond.

Bertram Charles, when discussing place names of the Oswestry area, was silent on *Maserfelth* and *Cocboy*. He stated too that 'the hitherto unidentified name *Llysfeisir* was the Welsh name of Maesbury, the old caput of the hundred: *Llesveyser* 1397 Ast[on Hall Deeds and Documents], "the *llys* or court of Meisyr", a female name which was also the name of the sister of Heledd in *Canu Llywarch Hen*'.[13] The Welsh form need not, however, be ancient, unlike *Maesbury* itself, from the Old English for 'border stronghold'. *Llysfeisir* may even be a late Welsh rendering or mistranslation of English *Maesbury*. On *Cocboy*, Kenneth Jackson translated Cynddelw's lines as 'When the man went to the battle of Cogwy in the conflict between the men of Powys and Oswald, son [*recte* brother] of Oswy.' (Cynddelw ignored Penda, the victor.) The anonymous verse, which Jackson took as perhaps of the ninth century, declares 'I saw armies on the ground of the field of Cogwy, and the battle full of affliction; Cynddylan was an ally.' Jackson believed that the latter proved Welsh participation in the battle, because Cynddylan ruled Powys at the time. On location, Jackson was categorical. 'The exact site of Cogwy cannot be identified.' Nor did he give any clue on what *Cogwy* meant, although it was nothing to do with *coch* (red).[14]

Sir Idris Foster repeated Ifor Williams's identification of *Cogwy* with *Maserfelth*, and maintained that 'Cynddylan was Penda's ally' there.[15] Enid Roberts went further. She asserted that Cynddylan, son of Cyndrwyn, is known to have been present at the battle of *Cogwy*, and that he was probably killed soon afterwards.[16] The Ordnance Survey nevertheless omits *Maserfelth* and

---

[10] Lewis 1942, 279.
[11] Rees 1951, plate 21.
[12] Hunter Blair 1954, 137–72.
[13] Charles 1963, 85–110.
[14] Jackson 1963b, 20–62.
[15] Foster 1965, 213–35.
[16] Roberts 1965, 20.

Cogwy from its maps.[17] However, Meisir daughter of Cyndrwyn does appear in Welsh genealogies, which locate her father's court at 'Lystin Wynnan' in the commote of Caereinion.[18] This last is the hilly district west of Welshpool. Later research moves 'Lystin Wynnan' from Caereinion to the commote of Cydewain immediately south of it. This clue on *Maserfelth*'s location is vital. It may be linked with Förster's suggestion, indirectly reported by Needham, on *Maserfelth* as an English translation of a Welsh form like *cae Meisir* (Meisir's field).[19]

Although Jackson thought that *Cogwy* could not be identified, Professor Kirby took *Maserfelth* as the stronghold of Old Oswestry, a mile north of the town.[20] A textbook glosses *Maserfeld* as 'probably Oswestry (= Oswald's Tree), Shropshire'.[21] Colgrave and Mynors observed that *Maserfelth* is generally identified as Oswestry.[22] Jackson thereafter cited the Welsh tradition that Cynddylan of Powys fought at Maserfelth in 642 and was killed by Penda.[23]

Margaret Gelling first voiced doubts on *Oswestry* and St Oswald in 1970. She noted that the form was unknown before the thirteenth century. Domesday calls the place *Meresberie* (boundary stronghold), now Maesbury, some two miles south of Oswestry. It had a church, and a later Shrewsbury Abbey charter proves that it was dedicated to St Oswald. He was certainly venerated in the region by the eleventh century. But it does not prove that he was killed there four centuries earlier. The Oswald associated with a tree at the spot may have been another person, and the site of *Maserfelth* another place.[24] The battlefield appears all the same (if with qualification) as Oswestry in paragraphs on seventh-century warfare.[25] Stenton, who dated the clash to 5 August 641, stated that *Maserfelth* was 'probably, though not certainly, to be identified with Oswestry. Nothing is recorded of the events which led up to the battle.'[26] Another took the defeat at a spot 'better known as Oswestry' as a failed Northumbrian attempt to split a Welsh-Mercian alliance.[27]

Name and place in ninth-century poems on Llywarch the Old and Heledd were surveyed by Sir Ifor Williams. They include Dwyriw (NGR SJ 0901), the

---

[17] *Map of Britain in the Dark Ages* 1966.
[18] Bartrum 1966, 60, 85.
[19] Needham 1966, 36.
[20] Kirby 1967, 58, 247.
[21] Whitelock 1967, 402.
[22] Colgrave and Mynors 1969, 242n.1.
[23] Jackson 1969, 62.
[24] Gelling 1970, 146–47.
[25] Alcock 1971, 340.
[26] Stenton 1971, 82.
[27] Finberg 1972, 383–532.

watersmeet of the rivers Rhiw in Montgomeryshire/Powys. (He noted the early form *rhyw* proved by rhyme, which implies a sense 'kind, sort'. The river's two branches were of different kinds. This etymology is more cogent than ones from *rhiw* (slope) or an unattested Welsh cognate of Latin *rivus* (river).) Dwyriw is two miles west of Bryn Cae Meisir (NGR SJ 1100), with the name of a Powys princess. Seven miles south-south-east is the River Meheli (NGR SO 1589), near the village of Kerry, where the Eagle of Eli swooped down and glutted itself on the flesh of dead warriors. The *Tren* (strong one) is the River Tern (NGR SJ 5509) of Shropshire, entering the Severn near Wroxeter and its Roman ruins. Eglwyseu Basa is Baschurch (NGR SJ 4222), eight miles north-west of Shrewsbury. (The Welsh name translates the English one and not vice versa.) A son of Llywarch was said to be buried at Llangollen, on the Upper Dee. These and other forms 'belong to the border districts from Kerry, Berriw [SJ 1800] up to Oswestry'.[28]

Assertion appears with John Morris, stating how Oswald 'was killed in 642 at Maes Cogwy, or Maeserfelth, that was thereafter renamed Oswestry'.[29] Hunter Blair hesitatingly linked *Maserfelth* with Oswestry.[30] Rachel Bromwich linked ninth-century poems from Powys to its seventh-century rulers.[31] As for Oswestry, Margaret Gelling continued to deny an original association of the spot with St Oswald.[32] Despite that, Peter Sawyer states that *Maserfelth* 'has been identified as Old Oswestry, a name that means "Oswald's tree", possibly in the sense of cross, for the Welsh form of the name is *Croesoswald*, "Oswald's Cross"', so attested in 1254.[33] The *Coccium* associated (wrongly) with *Cogwy* and explained (correctly) as 'red (river)' is taken as Edgeworth (NGR SD 7317), Lancashire, where local streams 'run red with iron'.[34] Professor Whitelock reproduced passages in the ninth-century *Historia Brittonum* on Penda, who 'fought the battle of *Cocboy*'. On Bede's account of the conflict she spoke of how *Maserfelth* = Oswestry 'derives support from Welsh poems that retain some memories of fighting in this area'.[35]

The most authentic of those poems, an elegy on Cynddylan of Powys dated by some to the seventh century, was edited by Geraint Gruffydd.[36] Further criticism by Margaret Gelling on Oswestry = *Maserfelth* indicates that Oswestry is

[28] Williams 1972, 149–50.
[29] Morris 1973, 241.
[30] Hunter Blair 1976, 45, 129.
[31] Bromwich 1978b, 321–22.
[32] Gelling 1978, 187.
[33] Sawyer 1978, 30.
[34] Rivet and Smith 1979, 310.
[35] Whitelock 1979, 263, 684.
[36] Gruffydd 1982, 10–28.

certainly 'Oswald's tree', but not that Oswald was the Northumbrian king or
the tree was a Christian cross.[37] Loyn states briefly that Oswald 'was killed on
campaign near Oswestry in 642'.[38] In a footnote, David Dumville expresses
doubts on many aspects of early Powys.[39] Wallace-Hadrill thought that
Maserfelth may have been Oswestry.[40]

Sir Ifor Williams's editorial work on the poetry of Llywarch the Old and
Heledd now appears in English. For our purposes there are two important
points. Among stanzas spoken by Princess Heledd is this one:

> The eagle of Eli: how grievous tonight
> Is the fine valley of Meisir (*Diffrynt Meissir*).
> The land of Brochfael has been long afflicted.

In a stray verse added to the original series, Heledd refers to *Maserfelth* and
laments Cynddylan, her brother.

> I saw on the ground of the field of Cogwy (*maes Cogwy*)
> Armies and battle affliction.
> Cynddylan was an ally.

Now, we have seen Eli taken as the River Meheli south-east of Newtown,
Powys. Meisir has been related to Bryn-cae-meisir (NGR SJ 1100) eight miles
west-south-west of Welshpool. As for Brochfael, he was a sixth-century Powys
ruler, so his 'land' is antonomasia for 'Powys'. Commenting on the first stanza,
Jenny Rowland cites a paper of the local historian J. P. Brown, in a 1978 issue
of *Y Faner*, the Welsh-language newspaper. He regarded 'Lystin Wynnan' or
Llystinwennan, home of Cyndrwyn, the father of Cynddylan and his sisters
Heledd and Meisir, as modern Stingwern (NGR SO 1399), by Stingwern Hill
(1,174 feet). Stingwern is a mile from Bryn-cae-meisir. Citing correspondence
with Margaret Gelling, Dr Rowland concludes in the light of this that Dyffryn
Meisir 'is best sought with the complex of names in latter-day Powys', and not
near Oswestry. This helps us with *Maserfelth*, 'almost universally identified as
Oswestry'.[41] Catherine McKenna of Harvard comments on how Cynddelw's
eulogy of St Tysilio praises his foundation at Meifod (NGR SJ 1513) for sanc-
tity and the excellence of its mead.[42] Her edition, with translation of the

---

[37] Gelling 1984, 212–16.
[38] Loyn 1984b, 5–18.
[39] Dumville 1988, 1–16.
[40] Wallace-Hadrill 1988, 102, 103.
[41] Rowland 1990, 123, 589.
[42] McKenna 1991, 31.

poem into English, is more accessible than that by others, with apparatus and modern rendering entirely in Welsh.[43] In 1993, Nick Higham of Manchester suggested that *Maserfelth* or *Maes Cogwy* was 'possibly Wigan (? Roman *Coccium*) in Makerfield, on the north side of the Mersey frontier'.[44] This even though Jackson in 1963 dismissed the identification as 'impossible philologically and doubtless historically too', and Rivet and Smith in 1979 located *Coccium* at Edgeworth, on the moors north of Bolton, Lancashire. In 1995 he said the same again.[45]

In that year appeared an extended account by Clare Stancliffe. Despite rejecting Kenyon and Higham's view of *Maserfelth* as Makerfield, Lancashire, she concluded that the 'way lies open for the identification of Oswestry and *Maserfelth*, though we must recognize that the case for identifying the two is not proven beyond a peradventure'. This is correct. Despite the declaration that 'it will, I think, be conceded that the arguments in favour of identifying *Maserfelth* and Oswestry are strong', not one of those advanced holds water.[46]

A note on the Peterborough Chronicle entry for 641, on Oswald's death at *Maserfeld*, cites Dr Stancliffe as contender for Oswestry as the battlefield, and Mrs Gelling as her main opponent.[47] Professor Charles-Edwards in 2001 cautiously put the battlefield at 'a site lying in between the Mercian territories and those of the Welsh'.[48] More roundly, the English Place-Name Society dictionary declares: 'In reality, however, the site and the identification of *Maserfelth* remain quite unknown.'[49] André Crépin all the same stated that Oswald 'fut tué par Penda' at Oswestry.[50] The crossed swords of battle at *Cocboy* similarly appear by Oswestry in a recent atlas.[51] For these commentators, the informed and coherent reasoning of Margaret Gelling counted for nothing.

Chris Lewis offers pertinent remarks. 'It is impossible to be sure in any formal sense that *Maserfelth* was Oswestry. Bede himself may not have known where it was.' Then, perceptively, 'The first part of *Maserfelth* could well be an obscure Welsh district name (perhaps garbled by Bede).' In any case, it is 'probable that *Maserfelth* was another territorial name in *feld*, with an unexplained first element which might conceivably be its earlier Welsh name'. Finally, 'it seems reasonable to suppose that *Maserfelth* was a Welsh territory controlled

---

[43] Jones and Owen 1991–95, I, 15–50.
[44] Higham 1993, 88.
[45] Higham 1995, 221, 255.
[46] Stancliffe 1995, 84–96.
[47] Swanton 1996, 27.
[48] Charles-Edwards 2001, 89–105.
[49] Watts 2004, 455.
[50] Crépin and Lapidge 2005b, 58.
[51] Koch 2007, map 22.

by an Anglo-Saxon king', like the hundred of Archenfield south of Hereford, where *Archen-* is from *Erging*, the region's Welsh name.[52] On *Croesoswallt*, Richard Morgan cites Margaret Gelling.[53] James Fraser sets the events of 5 August 642 'at a place conventionally identified as Oswestry in Shropshire'.[54] Tim Clarkson puts them 'somewhere in the English Midlands at the unlocated battlefield of *Maserfelth*'.[55] Clare Stancliffe still thinks the spot is 'probably to be identified as Oswestry'.[56] Professor Charles-Edwards asserts that Oswald 'died in battle against an alliance of Mercians and Britons at *Maserfelth*, Old Welsh *Cocboy*, the modern Oswestry close to the modern border of Wales.'[57] Nancy Edwards, in a volume often unreliable on dates and toponyms, asserts that Oswald 'was killed in a battle at Oswestry by an army which probably included the Welsh of Powys, but was led by Penda of Mercia.'[58] On whether the archaic elegy on Cynddylan (which alludes to *maes Cogwy*) dates from the seventh century or is much later, John Koch of Aberystwyth sides with the first or 'authenticist' school.[59] That inspires confidence in it as a historical text. Tim Clarkson later described the battlefield as 'unidentified', but 'perhaps in the borderlands between southern Deira and north-east Mercia'.[60] More recently he declares the battle's location as 'unknown'.[61]

So, despite labours from 1896 to 2018, British scholarship remains divided. Yet some points are agreed on. Nobody has found a convincing English etymology for *Maser-*. We may thus (after Max Förster 85 years ago) seek a Welsh form to explain it, on the parallel of *Ircingafeld* or Archenfield in the *Anglo-Saxon Chronicle* for 918, where Welsh *Erging* appears in English guise. If we take this approach, *Dyffryn Meisir* (Meisir's Vale) in the laments of Princess Heledd may supply an answer. Let us turn to Welsh evidence for *Maserfelth*.

The stanzas uttered by Heledd, especially those on the Eagle of Eli, contain many names. Cyndrwyn's doomed son Cynddylan is linked with the 'field of Cogwy', which tallies with other evidence for him as ruling in the earlier seventh century. They refer as well to Eli, the 'valley of Meisir' and 'land of Brochfael', the Severn, 'two Rhiws', and Edeirnion. Heledd calls herself daughter of Cyndrwyn and sister of Meisir. The family relationship is

---

[52] Lewis 2007, 130–43.
[53] Morgan 2008, 204–16.
[54] Fraser 2009, 174.
[55] Clarkson 2010, 128.
[56] Stancliffe 2010, 69–83.
[57] Charles-Edwards 2013, 345, 391–92.
[58] Edwards 2013, 9.
[59] Koch 2013, 177–204.
[60] Clarkson 2014, 34.
[61] Clarkson 2018, 99.

clear.[62] Also helpful is a twelfth-century genealogy on other sons of Cyndrwyn, whose court was at Llystinwennan. It lists three of them: Elhaearn of Cegidfa, Llwchaearn of Cydewain, and Cynhaearn of Eiddonydd.[63] It is true that their genealogy was compiled three centuries later than the verses.[64] Yet we have even earlier evidence for Cynddylan in the shape of an elegy on him, its text difficult and corrupt, but with archaisms pointing to a seventh-century original, and a reference to his plundering the monastery of Lichfield and slaughtering its 'book-clutching monks'.[65]

Some of these toponyms have been mapped by Wendy Davies.[66] Given the dearth of early Powys records, her reasons for doing so are understandable. 'Such is the hunger for historical source materials for this region at this date that, even with the problems recognized, this poetry is frequently discussed as if relevant to the construction of history in this region in the first half of the seventh century.'[67] We can add to those mappings, offering grid references from the modern map. We have listed Eli, the valley of Meisir, land of Brochfael, Severn, two Rhiws, Edeirnion and the brothers Elhaearn of Cegidfa, Llwchaearn of Cydewain, and Cynhaearn of Eiddonydd. Passing from west to east we find Dwyriw (NGR SJ 0901), where the rivers Rhiw unite; Bryn Cae Meisir (NGR SJ 1100) (hill of Meisir's field); and Llystinwennan or Stingwern (NGR SO 1399), home of Cynddylan's father, Cyndrwyn. These places are within three miles of each other. The region was known as the land of Brochfael, and there is still a Llannerch Frochwel (NGR SJ 1910) (Brochfael's clearing) three miles north-west of Welshpool. It is a mile from Cegidfa or Guilsfield (NGR SJ 2211), with a parish church dedicated to St Aelhaiarn or Elhaearn, nephew to Cynddylan, Heledd and Meisir. Another saintly nephew, Llwchaearn, has his church and dedication at Llanllwchaiarn (NGR SO 1090), a mile north of Newtown. The parish is in the commote of Cydewain, which straddles the Upper Severn; and Cydewain is separated on its north side from Edeirnion by the River Rhiw. Also in Cydewain, in its southern part and with a bloodthirsty Eagle of Eli, is the River Meheli, flowing past Glanmeheli (NGR SO 1690). The exception of these three brothers is St Cynhaearn of Eiddonydd or Eifionydd, whose church is at Ynyscynhaearn (NGR SH 5538), by Portmadoc on Gwynedd's south coast.

---

[62] Jones 1911, 15–17.
[63] Wade-Evans 1944, 322.
[64] Williams 1944, 45–8.
[65] Parry 1955, 10–11.
[66] Davies 1982, 100.
[67] Higham 2002, 178.

Grid references make dry reading. But they provide secure evidence. They cluster in the commote of Cydewain and specifically its northern part, between the Severn and the Rhiw, where we find Bryn Cae Meisir (NGR SJ 1100) and Llystinwennan or Stingwern (NGR SO 1399). One was the court of Cynddylan's father, Cyndrwyn; the other has the name of his sister, Meisir. That brings us to the mysterious *Dyffryn Meisir* of Princess Heledd, who mentions it in the same breath as the Land of Brochfael. Clearly, it should be sought in Cydewain and its environs. Now, a *dyffryn* is literally a water-course or river-bed, although with a later meaning 'valley' or even 'vale'. Here one notes with interest the farm of Dyffryn (NGR SJ 2001) on the banks of the Severn. It is situated four miles south of Welshpool, a mile north of the junction of Rhiw and Severn, and six miles east of Bryn-cae-meisir. Dyffryn is in the parish of Berriw, like Bryn-cae-meisir. Dyffryn is, therefore, the obvious place to take as *Dyffryn Meisir* (vale of Meisir), and hence *Maserfelth* (open land of Maser). The reference is to the broad floodplain of the River Severn, with strategic fords giving access to central Wales. If, then, we seek the place that gave its name to *Maserfelth*, we shall find it in the vicinity of Dyffryn (the Welsh equivalent of Old English *felth*), on the floodplain of the river Severn west of Forden, Powys.

At this point, a comment on hydronyms. Another supposed sister of Cynddylan, Heledd and Meisir was Ffreuer, whose grave is said to be at Nantffreuer (stream of Ffreuer) (NGR SH 9840), in wild country near Bala, Gwynedd.[68] But, since *ffreu* means 'flood, torrent, flow', it may be that a prin-cess has been invented from a river name. The same may have happened with the Rhiw, where *Rhiw* is of disputed origin.[69] If the Rhiw was once called *Meisir*, that would explain Dyffryn as perhaps *Dyffryn Meisir*. The modern farm will be called after the nearby river. We may speculate further. Meisir may have been the Rhiw's Celtic nymph or goddess. That would explain why 'Princess Meisir' has so small a place in the genealogies, and none in historical records. She was perhaps never a princess of flesh and blood, but a purely legendary personage, conjured out of a place name, like the wizard Merlin or *Myrddin* of *Caerfyrddin*, Carmarthen.

Whether Meisir existed or not, she is still useful, because she provides an etymology for *Maserfelth*. Everyone accepts that the first element of *Ircingafeld* or Archenfield in the *Anglo-Saxon Chronicle* is from Welsh *Erging*. In the light of that, Bede's *Maserfelth* (open land of Maser) as a rendering of *Dyffryn Meisir* (vale of Meisir) would not be strange. We shall see below how the Primitive Welsh or seventh-century form for *Meisir* can be established, thereby strengthening

---

[68] Lloyd-Jones 1931–63, 511.
[69] Owen and Morgan 2007, 27.

the argument. A battle of *Maserfelth* in the vicinity of the farm at Dyffryn in any case accords with military geography. The Roman road from Wroxeter to Caersws, which exposed central Wales to attack from Mercia, passed the village of Forden to reach the cavalry fort of Forden Gaer (NGR SO 2098), mistakenly regarded as 'Lavobrinta' (which is instead surely a corruption of *Fl[umen] Sabrina* (River Severn)).[70] Evidence for seventh-century events may or may not be found in reports on an early hall close to it.[71] Nearer to Dyffryn is a castle mound (NGR SJ 2100) on the banks of the Severn, presumably guarding a strategic ford. In short, the region suggests a long history of fighting. A battlefield in the Severn valley accords as well with the miracles reported by Bede on information from the monks of Bardney. A major route from Wales to England, with an inn nearby, is an apt place for the British wayfarers and other travellers mentioned by him. Remoter Bryn-cae-meisir, far from Roman roads, can be ruled out. No army or traveller would come there. The same, we may add, can be said of Oswestry itself, near no Roman road, and so no place for any Mercian or Northumbrian general who wanted mobility for his infantry. Let us say the same again. The road travelled by Oswald, Penda, and their armies, as also the travellers in Bede's stories of miracles, will be the Roman one near Welshpool. This in turn eliminates the claims of Oswestry, which lay on no ancient road, Roman or other.

If it is accepted that *Maserfelth* and *Dyffryn Meisir* were one, and can be identified with the plain by the farm of Dyffryn, on the banks of the Severn and near a major Roman road, it informs us as well on sound changes in Primitive Welsh. Jackson believed that Welsh internal *i*-affection, whereby preceding *a* was raised to *ei*, took place in 'the seventh or eighth century', but thought that more precise dating was not possible, although it was earlier in Welsh than in Cornish and Breton (where it occurred in the eighth century).[72] *Maser-* provides fresh evidence. The form being known to the English in 642, it shows that internal *i*-affection had not then taken place in Welsh. Bede would otherwise have written 'Meiserfelth' or 'Meisirfelth'.

There remains the problem of *Cocboy* or *Maes Cogwy*. It has at present neither location nor etymology. Nevertheless, Welsh *cogwrn* (lump, boss, knob, cone; knuckle, joint; limpet, periwinkle) perhaps comes to our aid.[73] It has been related to early Irish *coch* (rear part, behind) and Breton *cogell* (hillock), all from a reconstructed Common Celtic root *kok-*.[74] These allow us to take the first

---

[70] Houlder 1974, 95.
[71] Blockley 1990, 17–46.
[72] Jackson 1953, 611–12, 697.
[73] *Geiriadur Prifysgol Cymru* 1950–2002, 541.
[74] Vendryes 1987, 138.

element of *Cocboy* or *Cogwy* as 'cone, hillock' or the like. If it is objected that such an interpretation of *Coc-* has no parallel in Welsh and other toponymy, we may answer that perhaps it has, but the element has not been recognized for what it is. This means a further excursion into Celtic philology.

In south-west Scotland, four miles north-east of Sanquhar on the Dumfries-Kilmarnock railway, is Cog Burn (NGR NS 8213), with the farms of Nether Cog and Upper Cog by its foot and Cogshead near its source. Watson explained it as Gaelic *cóig* (five) for *cóigeamh* (fifth (part)), on the analogy of other places in Scotland.[75] He did not consider that it might instead be Cumbric, as with nearby Orchard (= Welsh *Argoed* ([place] by a wood)) or Corsbank (compare Welsh *cors* (fen, bog)). More evidence comes from Wales and the obscure form *Cogan*. On the southern fringe of Cardiff is Cogan, with Cogan Pill running past it into Penarth Docks. Two miles south of it (and east of Barry) is the hamlet of Cog, on a hilltop and looking north to Cog Moors, former marshland. A confident explanation of all these from Old Danish *kog* (piece of marshland (lately reclaimed)) is doubted in a classic work on Welsh hydronyms, in part because it does not account for the names of Glyncogan (NGR SJ 1303), near Welshpool in Powys; Cogan, a brook (NGR SO 0891) west of Newtown, Powys; Castell Cogan (NGR SN 1314), a hillfort six miles south-west of Carmarthen; and Chapelle de Les-Cogan (where *les* = Welsh *llys* (court)), Brittany. The same goes for attempts to relate them to Welsh *cawg* (bowl, basin), especially for the hamlet of Cog, which is not in a hollow but on top of a hill.[76]

These forms do not relate to Danes, marshlands (reclaimed or not) or basins. We are instead dealing with toponyms of different origins, which deserve a study in their own right. What concerns us here are Cog Burn in Scotland, Glyncogan and Nant Cogan in Powys, Cog and Cogan in Glamorgan and perhaps Castell Cogan in Carmarthenshire. All are in hilly or rocky regions. On this basis our proposed link with the element common to Welsh *cogwrn* (lump, boss, knob, cone), Irish *coch* (rear part, behind) and Breton *cogell* (hillock) (in the names of Ar Gogell, Park Ar Gogell, Lann Gogell and with the variant *Kogenn*) may stand. In Glamorgan, Cog is on the crest of a wide hill, Cogan by a small one (pierced by a railway tunnel), so that they might be regarded as 'hill' and 'hillock' (with diminutive suffix *-an*), respectively. As for Cog Burn, Glyncogan and Nant Cogan, the sense will be that they adjoin hills. Cog Burn runs between large ones, going up to nearly 2,000 feet; Glyncogan and Nant Cogan by smaller ones. Castell Cogan likewise crowns a hill, a conspicuous one. If *Cocboy* denoted yet another Brittonic hill, there would apparently be no

---

[75] Watson 1926, 185.
[76] Thomas 1938, 57–58.

difficulty. (That Cog Burn should instead be referred to Welsh *cog* (cuckoo), like Blencogow (height of cuckoos) in north-west Cumbria, is not credible. The bleak heights around it were no place for cuckoos.)

Now for -*boy*. It can be related to the names of Welshmen called Rhonabwy, Gwenabwy, Cynabwy or Hunabwy.[77] There is a closer parallel in the first part of the Brittonic personal name *Boia*. In the tenth century a Cornish deacon called Boia witnessed the manumission of slaves, recorded in the Bodmin Gospels. In Wales was another Boia, an evil chieftain who persecuted St David. His name still appears on the map at Clegyr Fwya (Boia's Rock), a neolithic and Iron Age site west of the cathedral at St Davids.[78] The same element appears in the Old Welsh personal names *Conuoe* and *Guoruoe* (later *Gwrfwy*), with initial elements meaning 'hound' and 'man', respectively.[79] There is also a lost name *Conuoy* near Pontarddulais in west Glamorgan, perhaps referring to a stream, where the sense 'strike' (on the basis of Welsh *bwyall* (axe)) has been proposed for -*uoy*.[80] At first sight one might link -*boy*, -*uoy* or -*fwy* to -*abwy* in the Welsh personal names *Gwenabwy*, *Iunabwy* (as at Llandinabo (church of Iunabwy), near Hereford), *Rhonabwy* and the like, which might be related to early Welsh *abwy* (prey).[81] On that basis, *Cocboy* or *Cogwy* may be understood as 'hill of prey, outcrop where prey was found', implying the same semantic range as (for example) Cyfarthfa (place of barking, place where hunted animals were at bay) near Merthyr Tudful.[82] But there is surely a far better explanation in *Verbeia*, the British-Latin name of the River Wharfe, Yorkshire, with a form apparently meaning 'great striker' and so related to Welsh *bwyall* (axe).

However its name is interpreted, we can indicate exactly where this hill was. The farm of Dyffryn is the parish of Berriw. Immediately to the east, beyond the Severn, is Forden. In an account of it, a nineteenth-century topographer remarked that just by Offa's Dyke, 'on the road from Welshpool to Montgomery, rises a vast conoidal rock, upon which, on clearing away the surface, after the middle of the last century, the remains of a fort were discovered'. He commented further: 'The history of this place is involved in total oblivion: it was probably a fortification of considerable importance, as it commanded the line of Offa's Dyke, and the vales of Severn, Montgomery and Chirbury: at a short distance from it is another intrenchment.'[83] Fortunately,

---

[77] Evans 1988, 46.
[78] Davies 1979, 158, 169.
[79] Thomas 1933–35, 117–33.
[80] Williams 1939–41, 36–44.
[81] Richards 1948, 29.
[82] Williams 1945, 32.
[83] Haslam 1979, 103.

we now know more. The castle was built on 'a tall natural outcrop' (NGR SO 2301) in about 1260 by the Corbets of Shropshire, only to be destroyed by the Welsh in 1263.[84] The phrases 'vast conoidal rock' and 'tall natural outcrop' go well with the reconstructed root Celtic *kok-* seen in Welsh *cogwrn* (lump, boss, knob, cone; knuckle, joint) and Breton *cogell* (hillock). In short, this conspicuous landmark seems to be *Cocboy* or *Cogwy* (hill of *Boia* 'striker'?), on the borders of Mercia and Powys, above a strategical Roman road, and less than two miles east of the farm of Dyffryn related to *Dyffryn Meisir* or *Maserfelth*.

Our dossier is complete. The evidence in it suggests that the battle of *Maserfelth*, fought on 5 August 642, was in the parishes of Berriw and Forden, Montgomeryshire, Powys. The latter contains a conspicuous craggy landmark that might be called *Cocboy* or 'Boia's Rock'. The Roman road from Wroxeter to central Wales bisects it. Because place-name scholars explain *Forden* from the Old English for 'highway settlement', it is a suitable place for the inn and Welsh or other travellers of Bede, as it is on the main route from mid-Wales to the Midlands. We may also regard it as near where Penda, more grimly, left Oswald's head and arms on display as roadside trophies. These were recovered after a year by a Northumbrian force, presumably moving along Roman roads via Manchester, Whitchurch and Wroxeter, giving a wide berth to the Mercian capital at Tamworth, near Lichfield. We may say again that Forden is bounded to the west by the River Severn; on the further bank, in the parish of Berriew, is Dyffryn, apparently *Dyffryn Meisir* (vale of Meisir). Finally, Forden is some nine miles south-east of Meifod (NGR SJ 1513), where St Tysilio was abbot, and Mathrafal (NGR SJ 1310), where Powys princes held court (substantial earthworks of their castle remain). It is no surprise if, when the bard Cynddelw in the twelfth century sang praise to Tysilio, he should have mentioned the battle of *Cogwy*, fought at a spot less than a morning's walk from his monastery.

We end with four conclusions. First, if historians accept that *Maserfelth* was fought between Mercians and Northumbrians in August 642 at Forden, two miles from Wales's modern border with England, it will vindicate Max Förster, who long ago linked *Maserfelth* and the Welsh princess Meisir, and Margaret Gelling, who consistently denied the claims of Oswestry to be the place. Second, it is strange that Förster's proposal remained unnoticed (except by Needham in 1966) in the English-speaking world; even if Chris Lewis in 2007 had independently come to a similar conclusion. Third, it demonstrates the historical uses of place-name analysis.

Finally, and for the benefit for battlefield archaeologists, can we be more exact on where combat took place? We have certain clues. Bede's two miracle

---

[84] Haslam 1978.

stories indicate a site close to Wales but not in it; on a highway; and near a village to which a paralytic girl (brought thence by cart and cured at the spot where Oswald fell) could return on foot. It is hard to avoid the conclusion that the village was Forden, now in Wales, but with an English name meaning 'settlement by a route'. The name itself accords with Bede's statement that the girl's uncle ran an inn (*hospitium*) in the village. Forden owes its existence to the Roman road; Bede's anonymous village was a place where wayfarers stayed. As for the detail of how the girl (having 'washed her face, arranged her hair and covered her head with a linen kerchief') walked back home, miraculously recovered, this may indicate a locality within a mile or less of the settlement. If there is anything in identification of *Cocboy* with Castle Mound, and *Maes Cogwy* as the open ground near it, that puts the battlefield east of Forden and not by the Roman fort to the south-west (nor does Bede mention any fortification). Nevertheless, archaeological opinion on vegetation at the time, earthworks by the Wroxeter road and possible occupation of Forden Gaer will here be crucial. In a few years, fieldwork and perhaps finds from the seventh century may confirm the arguments set out here for *Maserfelth* as fought in August 642 in the vicinity of Forden, bordering the Welsh district of *Dyffryn Meisir* (vale of Meisir).

Chapter 10

655: TREASURE LOST ON THE *UINUED* OR RIVER WENT, YORKSHIRE

The Battle of the *Uinued* in 655, debated by scholars for over four centuries, is now understood thus. After a humiliating capitulation at Stirling, where he had to hand over fabulous amounts of treasure, Oswiu (d. 670) of Northumbria pursued the victorious Penda to the *Uinued* near Leeds, killed him and gained power over Mercia until his death. Oswiu's triumph showed a sensational reversal of fortune. Yet aspects of it remain unclear. What follows thus has four parts. It surveys discussion of the battle, offers an etymology for its name, suggests where it was fought and proposes a new account of it based on this material.

Bede says the battle took place 'near the river *Uinued*, which had broken its banks after heavy rain, so that far more were drowned as they tried to run away than died by the sword in combat'. Plummer has a useful commentary here, citing authorities from Camden onwards. He notes that the Old English Bede translates as *neah Winwede streame*; rejects the view that this was in Lothian; explains the name as an English one, the second element meaning 'ford' and the first perhaps meaning 'fight' (this is impossible); and describes its location as obscure. Plummer, an Anglican priest, also notes how the battle meant the effective end of Anglo-Saxon paganism. Besides its political consequences, it was hence 'decisive as to the religious destiny of the English'.[1] Anderson, although rightly cool on the idea that there were Celts from Cornwall, Ireland and Scotland in the Northumbrian army, notes that Oswiu's nephew Talorcen, son of Eanfrith, was the Pictish King. So Pictish warriors may have fought by the *Uinued*.[2] Against this, however, is Bede's statement that Oswiu's army was 'tiny'. His victory was, like Waterloo, surely won by choice of battlefield, not superiority in numbers.

The *Uinued*, figuring in almost all accounts of Anglo-Saxon England, also appears in histories of Wales. Sir John Lloyd (locating it in the West Riding)

---

[1] Plummer 1896, II, 183–84.
[2] Anderson 1908, 25n.2.

describes it characteristically. After Penda's triumph at Stirling, he tells how Oswiu at Winwaed Field burst upon his 'serried hosts' who were returning in 'careless mood' and 'slew the implacable enemy of his house'. He adds that the conflict appears in Welsh annals as the slaughter of Campus Gai (the field of Caius), and that *Historia Brittonum* tells how Penda's ally Cadafael (whose name means 'battle-seizer') of Gwynedd deserted him the night before, thereby gaining the nickname *Cadomedd* 'battle-shunner'. Yet Lloyd, a Welsh patriot, is careful to state that 'among the thirty noble leaders who fell around Penda there must have been no small number of Britons, the last of their race seriously to contest with the English the supremacy of the isle of Britain'. (Welsh blood washed out the stain of treachery.) More fundamentally, Lloyd points out that the victory not only made Oswiu 'supreme ruler of Britain', but marked off the Cumbrians from the Welsh for ever. The division between the Britons of Wales and those of Cumbria and Strathclyde became irrevocable. In 655, Wales hence began existence as a separate nation.[3] For Lloyd and his successors, the *Uinued* was a battle of epoch-making significance.[4]

A detailed account of the conflict was given by Hunter Blair. He noted the contradictions between the accounts of Penda's last campaign in Bede and in *Historia Brittonum*, observing Bede does not actually say that Penda died on the *Uinued* (and that his death is placed by *Annales Cambriae* in the year after the battle). Hunter Blair, regarding the *Uinued* as being near Leeds and flowing into the Humber, pointed out that Bede says nothing of Welsh participation there. As for *Historia Brittonum*, he saw difficulties in reconciling Oswiu's capitulation on the Forth described there with a triumph immediately after near Leeds. Were there two separate campaigns? He further stated that the site of *Campus Gai*, the name of the battle in *Historia Brittonum* and the Welsh annals, was unknown. Yet there was no doubt of the victory's importance for Northumbrian supremacy.[5]

Alhough it is now rejected, Stenton made a stimulating suggestion on the *Uinued* and Sutton Hoo. Penda had killed Anna, King of East Anglia, but his brother fought and died as Penda's ally on the *Uinued*. Because little is known of this brother, Stenton proposed that after a shattering defeat his body perhaps remained in Northumbrian hands. There was hence 'nothing to forbid the perpetuation of his name by a great memorial, nor is there anything alien to the feeling of his age in the surrender of his treasure to the earth'.[6] Even if Stenton's conjecture must be discarded, following dating to about 625 of coins

[3] Lloyd 1911, 190–91.
[4] Williams 1941, 78, 79, 81, 97.
[5] Hunter Blair 1954, 163–65.
[6] Stenton 1959.

from Sutton Hoo and evidence that the mound did contain a body, it offers a lesson in the inspired use of historical evidence.

Henry Loyn avoided Lloyd's rhetoric, yet noted how Penda's successes depended on active support from Welsh princes, some of whom died at 'Winwaed Heath'.[7] As for Hunter Blair's doubts, these were in part cleared up by Jackson. Quoting *Historia Brittonum* for the death of Penda and all his British allies (except Cadafael of Gwynedd) *in campo Gai*, he described this and the *Uinued* as unidentified, but argued strongly that Oswiu's humiliation by Penda took place at Stirling (not elsewhere in Scotland), Oswiu thereafter fighting Penda near Leeds and destroying him and his army. Jackson also corrected the explanation of Cadafael's name and nickname. *Cadafael* actually means 'battle prince', which *Historia Brittonum* alters to (in Old Welsh orthography) *Catgabail* (battle-taking) (which would sound almost the same), with the derisive epithet *Catguommed* (battle-shunning) added.[8]

There was a fundamental step in 1966, when the Ordnance Survey (OS) located the *Uinued* where the Roman road north-west of Doncaster crosses the River Went.[9] This escaped most historians, who carried on describing the battlefield as at an unknown spot near Leeds. Kirby, locating the *Uinued* near Leeds, nevertheless made the point that routes across the Pennines from north-west and south-west converged there, so that the area had strategic importance.[10] Sherley-Price took a step forward by hesitantly identifying the *Uinued* as the Went, Yorkshire.[11] Colgrave and Mynors, declaring the river to be unidentified, merely followed Hunter Blair on it as a tributary of the Humber.[12] Although not mentioning the *Uinued*, Alcock refers to Penda's seige of Oswiu at Stirling as demonstrating the unusual mobility of armies in this period.[13] Stenton described the battlefield as an unknown spot somewhere near Leeds; his editors thought possible a link with Sutton Hoo.[14] Despite Jackson's arguments, Hunter Blair retained the hypothesis that Penda led not one but two campaigns into Northumbria, since he spoke of his leading an army against Oswiu. He did not think Oswiu attacked Penda from the rear as he retreated from Stirling, weighed down with treasure. Following Bede and *Annales Cambriae*, he observed too that the King of East Anglia was killed in the conflict and Penda also died there or soon after.[15]

---

[7] Loyn 1962, 34.
[8] Jackson 1963b.
[9] *Map of Britain in the Dark Ages.*
[10] Kirby 1967, 246.
[11] Sherley-Price 1968, 264.
[12] Colgrave and Mynors 1969, 257n.3.
[13] Alcock 1971, 338.
[14] Stenton 1971, 51, 84.
[15] Hunter Blair 1977, 51.

Bromwich comments on Cadafael's ill-fame in Welsh tradition. A triad in the fourteenth-century White Book of Rhydderch calls him one of the three kings descended from churls. With the description of him as 'battle-dodger' in the ninth-century *Historia Brittonum*, his absence from Welsh genealogies and his general historical obscurity, he was probably a usurper who failed to establish a dynasty.[16] Hence, perhaps, his need for an alliance with Penda. Had his line survived, tradition might instead have praised his political deftness or adroitness in deserting an ally at the right time. So the *Uinued* has its own fame in Welsh sources.

Sawyer made brief but fundamental points here. Although uncertain if Penda took the treasure that Oswiu offered him, he is sure that Penda rewarded his allies freely. Despite this, Penda was eventually defeated on the *Uinued*, an unidentified river near Leeds, on 15 November 655. (The date is vital evidence.) Oswiu thereupon became overlord of Mercia.[17] Whitelock provides translations of the relevant passages in the Chronicle, *Historia Brittonum*, and Bede; and declares that the site of the battlefield 'cannot be located' but was (according to Bede) near Leeds.[18] It is still absent from Hill's map of toponyms in Bede.[19]

Later historians vary in the importance they give the *Uinued*. Campbell, setting out the 'sparse and bloody tale' of seventh-century kingship, simply observes that, while Penda had killed Anna of East Anglia, Anna's brother and successor was killed by Northumbrians while fighting for Penda at the battle of the *Winwaed* in 655.[20] In an admirable study, Wendy Davies does not refer to the battle at all, although she refers to alliances between Penda and Gwynedd kings as signs of Anglo-Welsh cooperation.[21] Her failure to mention the battle contrasts with Lloyd's emphasis in 1911 on its dramatic reversal of fortune and its implications for the birth of the Welsh nation. However, Henry Loyn spoke of Northumbria's 'most impressive lordship' over the English after Penda's defeat. Although this domination was relatively short-lived (as early as 658 the Mercians revolted against and expelled ealdormen from the North), the Northumbrian decision at Whitby in 664 to accept the customs of the Roman Church meant it was these, and not Celtic custom, that prevailed throughout England.[22] A battle, marking the opening of Northumbria's golden age, had

---

[16] Bromwich 1978b, 179, 289–90, 546.
[17] Sawyer 1978, 31.
[18] Whitelock 1979, 164, 263, 693–94.
[19] Hill 1981, 30.
[20] Campbell 1982, 56.
[21] Davies 1982, 113.
[22] Loyn 1984, 9, 25.

theological consequences. Wallace-Hadrill (following J. O. Prestwich) thinks textual corruption may explain Bede's curious attribution of Penda's war to an East Anglian king, and (following Dumville) doubts whether a North British history was incorporated wholesale into *Historia Brittonum*'s text.[23]

Higham makes some fresh points on the campaign. He thinks Bede's terminology of 30 *legiones* led by *duces regi* and so on owes more to Bede's numerology and perceptions of Roman authority than historical fact. He also considers Penda may have needed a guarantee of East Anglian support (besides that of Welsh princes) before he could attack Northumbria.[24] Swanton, describing 'Winwidfeld' as 'unidentified', accepts it may have been by a tributary of the Humber.[25] On Sutton Hoo an official guide now cites datings of about 625 for the coins there, so there is nothing against taking the grave as Redwald's; excavators found no body there because it had been dissolved by the acids of sandy soil (though still leaving tell-tale phosphate traces).[26] That eliminates a link with an East Anglian king at *Uinued* 30 years later. As regards the battle, there is a brief one by Charles-Edwards, who states that Cadafael of Gwynedd was Penda's ally there, and that the conflict took place 'close to Leeds'.[27]

This concludes the first part of this paper. The historical sources, though sparse. still provide a thick dossier of material, with differences of emphasis, contradictions and repetition. Yet there is more to say. If we could be sure where the battle was fought, it would sharpen our focus on this event, with consequences for the whole of Britain.

What does philology tell us about Bede's *Uinued?* There is no problem with the first element, which represents Brittonic 'white', as in Welsh *gwyn* (white). This has parallels at Wynford (white torrent) (National Grid Reference (NGR) SY 5895) in Dorset and Wendover (white water) in Buckinghamshire.[28] As for the second element, a solution is indicated by the Ravenna Cosmography's *Coccuveda* (the River Coquet, Northumberland), which is directly related to Welsh *cochwedd* (redness; red appearance). Richmond and Crawford observed that the Coquet is 'filled with red porphyritic detritus from the Cheviot', so that it is a 'red river' like many others, including the Río Tinto or the Llobregat (derived from *Rubricatum*) of Spain.[29] If the Coquet was the river of 'redness', the *Uinued* could be the river of 'whiteness'.

---

[23] Wallace-Hadrill 1988, 121, 234.
[24] Higham 1995, 25, 55, 66, 172.
[25] Swanton 1996, 29.
[26] Carver 1998, 34–35.
[27] Charles-Edwards 2001, 93.
[28] Coates and Breeze 2000, 295, 363.
[29] Rivet and Smith 1979, 311.

Two points may be mentioned on the philology involved here. First, since the *e* of *-wedd* was raised from *i* in the earlier fifth century by affection from following long *a*, the *e* of Ravenna's *Coccuveda* is probably due to the regular late Latin confusion of *i* and *e*.[30] Second, an interpretation of *Uinued* as 'whiteness; white aspect' is confirmed by Middle Welsh *gwenwedd* (whiteness) (with feminine first element) in a poem of carousal by Dafydd ap Gwilym, who (significantly) applies it to a *ffrwd* (torrent).[31] His reference to liquid sheds light on this river name in Bede.

If the Coquet was the river of 'redness', Oswiu and Penda fought by the river of 'whiteness' or 'white appearance'. This was surely the Yorkshire Went (recorded as *Weneta* on the OS Map for this period, with lowering of the first vowel by assimilation), which flows sixteen miles eastwards to enter the Don seven miles south of Goole. That pinpoints the battlefield. It also makes strategic sense. Roman engineers avoided the marshes at the head of the Humber, so that until modern times there were only two main land routes south out of Yorkshire. One led south-east from York and crossed the Humber at Ferriby; the other went south-west to Tadcaster and then south via Doncaster to Lincoln. The dangers for a retreating army of the first, with a major river-crossing by boat, are obvious. Penda would naturally take the second route, meeting his doom where the road crossed the Went in former marshland. This would be at a point (NGR SE 4716) one mile west of modern Wentbridge and eleven miles north-west of Doncaster, or else (the road dividing a mile north of the Went) a thousand yards further west (NGR SE 4616).

The Went has a strange course. Its headwaters are in flat open land, but to the east of Wentbridge it runs through a narrow valley before reaching the marshlands of the lower Don. Even in the Middle Ages the Roman road striking across the Went's upper plain would have been hazardous in winter, so that early travellers soon kept to the drier rising ground east of it on the road via Wentbridge (where a *pons de Wenet* is known even in the twelfth century). Hence Penda's troubles.

Bede's *prope fluuium Uinued pugnatum est* almost certainly locates the battlefield north of the two sites (in NGR SE 4616 and 4716) where the Roman route south crosses the Went. This apparently satisfies all the evidence. The battle occurred on 15 November when heavy rain had flooded the region. It needed no military genius to see that Penda's large army could be bottled up on the northern approaches to the bridges, which could be crossed only by a few men at a time. In conditions of panic and rout, many men tried to escape through the floods and were drowned, as Bede tells us. The Chronicle confirms this

---

[30] Jackson 1953, 573–78.
[31] Parry 1952, 351.

view, saying that Oswiu slew Penda *on Winwidfelda*, where *feld* means not 'field' but 'open country, land free from wood, plain', which well describes the flatlands of the upper Went. The sense 'open country' also appears in the *Campus Gai* of *Historia Brittonum* and the Welsh annals (where Gai or Gaius may have been a local Romano-British landowner, whose name was preserved by Welsh tradition).

Why, however, need the case for locating this conflict be made so strongly? Did the OS not place it in 1966 north of where the Tadcaster-Doncaster road bridges the Went? The answer must be that its work has effectively been ignored by almost all subsequent writers, including Colgrave and Mynors, Stenton, Sawyer, Whitelock, Hill, Swanton and Charles-Edwards. So the point needs to be made clearly that there is reason to think that Oswiu's defeat of Penda took place on 15 November 655, after a period of heavy rain, on the northern approaches to the Roman crossing of the Went, south of the modern village of East Hardwick.

If this reasoning is accepted, how does it change our thinking? There seem four points here. We can rule out Hunter Blair's view that Penda was defeated while attacking Northumbria. No sane general would begin a major campaign in November, after bad weather had made roads impassable. We may readily accept Jackson's arguments that the defeat took place after a prolonged campaign in North Britain, when Penda was returning with treasure to Mercia. On this matter Hunter Blair followed Bede, who says that Penda refused the gold and silver, and not *Historia Brittonum*, on how he accepted it. Jackson observed that Bede is an accurate historian and the compiler of *Historia Brittonum* is not. But even Homer can nod. So we need not think of two consecutive Mercian campaigns in Northumbria. Penda was surely returning in late 655 after a single long campaign that had taken him as far north as Stirling.

A second question concerns the forces involved and Oswiu's generalship. Bede says that the Northumbrian army was so tiny that Penda's coalition was said to outnumber it thirty to one. In normal circumstances a Northumbrian victory would be out of the question. However, once the nature of the battle-field is grasped, a victory over much larger forces makes sense. Oswiu presumably took advantage of November flooding to trap Penda's army in front of the Went, which had broken its banks. Fighting downhill, the Northumbrians would have an advantage over an enemy with limited room for manoeuvre and no effective means of retreat. One assumes Oswiu chose the field with care and was richly rewarded. There are parallels with Agincourt and Waterloo, where intelligent use of terrain (Oswiu was also aided by weather) enabled smaller armies to defeat bigger ones.

Third, archaeology. *Historia Brittonum* tells how Oswiu handed all the riches he had in *Iudeu* (= Stirling) to Penda, who distributed it to the kings of the

British, so that it was known as the 'Restitution of Iudeu' (Old Welsh *Atbret Iudeu*, as explained by Jackson). This wealth, some of which came to Wales with Cadafael's astute retreat, must have been impressive. It would not otherwise be found in Welsh tradition 150 years later. Bede calls it 'an incalculable and incredible store of royal treasures and gifts', and Sutton Hoo (even though a link with *Uinued* must be ruled out) reminds us what an Anglo-Saxon king might dispose of. If we are right in placing the battle near the Went, treasure not recovered by Oswiu may still lie buried in its meadows, where professional archaeologists or others might find it, together with spearheads, buckles, items of harness and other military trappings.

A final small point. A few historians refer to the battle of *Uinued* without definite article. Since we have a river name, the article should be used, as with the Battles of the Nile, the Marne, the Somme, the Vistula, the Ebro and so on.

If, then, we are correct in locating the Battle of the *Uinued* on 15 November 655 upon open land between East Hardwick and the Went, we see more clearly a decisive battle of English history. Its drama needs no emphasis. Laden down with treasure after their triumph in North Britain, Penda's hosts were nearing the border of Mercia, where they found themselves trapped by floodwater at the wrong end of a causeway across marshes. The chaos of the scene, as thousands of men tried to flee along one narrow road, may be imagined. Penda's forces by the Went faced a predicament like that of Napoleon's armies by the Beresina on his retreat from Moscow, and by the Pleisse (where tens of thousands of men attempted escape across one small bridge) at the Battle of Leipzig. Small wonder that Bede saw such a crushing defeat, bringing Penda's downfall and the slaughter of 30 princes with him, as God's judgement on the wicked, with Oswiu thereafter *pro conlata sibi uictoria gratias Deo referens* (giving thanks to God for the victory he had given him), a result that to many Northumbrians must have seemed little short of miraculous.

The above was published in 2004.[32] Comment since then has included the following. In 2005, Crépin to his credit took the river of the battle as 'peut-être la Went, petit affluent de la Don'.[33] In 2007 James Fraser wrote of how on 15 November 655 'the superpowers met at *Maes Gai* on an unidentified river called *Winwaed* by Bede, in the district of Leeds (*Loidis*), probably in the orbit of the British kingdom of Rheged.'[34] His 'maes Gai' (*maes* 'field') is a form unknown to the sources. It is also hard to see why he calls the river 'unidentified' when the OS took it as the Went as far back as 1966. Nor, being

---

[32] Breeze 2004.
[33] Crépin and Lapidge 2005b, 137.
[34] Fraser 2007, 187.

north-west of Doncaster, was it anywhere near Rheged, with its heartland around Penrith, on the other side of the Pennines. In 2010 Tim Clarkson, in a detailed account, located the engagement on an 'unidentified' river near Leeds.[35] In 2013 Thomas Charles-Edwards (citing the *Northern History* paper) noted how the battlefield was first located on the Went by James Raine (1791–1858), Durham librarian and antiquary, although on this point Plummer was 'sceptical'.[36] One may yet reply that, although Plummer was a great scholar, he was wrong on *Uinued*, just as he was wrong on 'Degsastan', *Maserfelth*, *Brunanburh* and other places. Also from 2013 is Venning's useful handbook, where he describes the encounter as occurring 'probably near Leeds', going on to state that King Penda was among those 'cut down or drowned in the river'.[37] If so, it is curious that Bede, who loathed Penda for his worship of the old gods, says nothing on that.

In the second decade of the twenty-first century, there were those who would not accept the equation *Uinued* = Went, even when advances in Celtic philology show the proposal as sound. If, of course, amateur archaeologists or others now find on the banks of the Went some of Penda's treasure or other items from the conflict, such reluctance to accept what seems obvious might change abruptly.

---

[35] Clarkson 2010, 140.
[36] Charles-Edwards 2013, 394.
[37] Venning 2013, 55.

Chapter 11

844: *ALUTTHÈLIA*, VIKINGS, AND
A BRIDGE AT BISHOP AUCKLAND

'In the same year,' declares an annal of 844 preserved by Roger of Wendover, 'Aethelred, king of the Northumbrians, was expelled from the kingdom, and Raedwulf succeeded to the kingdom; and when, hastily invested with the crown, he fought a battle with the pagans at *Alutthèlia*, he and Ealdorman Alfred fell with a large part of their subjects, and then Aethelred reigned again.' The annal may relate to the entry for 844 in the Annals of St Bertin's, in part by Bishop Prudentius (d. 861) of Troyes, on how the Northmen then 'attacked with war the island of Britain, especially in the part which is inhabited by the Anglo-Saxons, and fighting for three days were victorious, committed plunder, rapine, and slaughter everywhere, and possessed the land at their pleasure'.[1]

The fatal events at *Alutthèlia* in 844 have not attracted much attention. Kirby, observing that Danish raids worsened in the 840s, referred to the death in 844 of Raedwulf of Northumbria in battle against the invader, linking what was relayed by Roger to the words of Prudentius.[2] Roger's annal was also noted by Stenton. He spoke of it as rare evidence for Northumbrian history at this date, showing how the kingdom suffered from Viking attacks, like the rest of England. The perceptive comment is also made that, although Raedwulf is mentioned in no other historical document, his name occurs on many Anglo-Saxon coins in the British Museum and elsewhere. It indicates a stronger and more significant ruler than manuscript sources would imply. The shortness of his reign ('hastily invested with the crown') can probably be reconciled with this. An energetic usurper might well issue many coins rapidly.[3]

In any case, we should no doubt hear more from modern historians on the battle of 844 if we knew where *Alutthèlia* was. Whitelock observed that, unless the form is very corrupt, it cannot represent *Elvet* (Swan Stream) (on the River Wear opposite Durham), which appears in the Anglo-Saxon Chronicle for 762

---

[1] Whitelock 1979, 282, 343.
[2] Kirby 1967, 76.
[3] Stenton 1971, 244.

as *Ælfetee*.[4] This must be right. So there seems a case for identifying *Alutthèlia* with Bishop Auckland, eight miles south-south-west of Durham. (Because 'Bishop', alluding to the Bishop of Durham, dates from after the Norman Conquest, we shall call it 'Auckland'.) The evidence can be set out thus.

Auckland has a Celtic name, recorded as *Alclit* in about 1050 and *Aucland* in 1254 (where it has been assimilated to Old Norse *Aukland* (additional land)). *Alclit* is explained as the exact equivalent of Cumbric *Al Clut* (rock on the Clyde), the old name of Dumbarton (= Gaelic *Dún mBreatainn* (hillfort of the Britons)) in Scotland, where a British stronghold crowned a basalt volcanic plug by the Clyde. At Auckland the river is now the Gaunless (from Old Norse *gagnlauss* (useless, unprofitable), perhaps because it was unfit for navigation, or else lacking in fish). But the Gaunless may once have been called 'Clyde', meaning 'purger, cleanser'. If so, 'hill on the Clyde, hill on the cleansing river' would be an apt name for Auckland.[5] Here we may quote Leland. He said of the town, 'It standith on a pratty hille bytwene two ryvers, wherof Were lyith on the north side, and Gaunless on the south and an arow shot or more beneth they meete and make one stream, and ren to the este. And ech of these rivers hath an hille by it, so that Bissop Castelle Akeland stadith on a litle hille bytwixt two greate hills.'[6]

Auckland was, therefore, on a natural defensive site by a river that was apparently once called 'Clyde'. Is our ninth-century *Alutthèlia* relevant to this? It seems that it is. It resembles forms of similar date for the name of Dumbarton. The fortress there appears in Old Welsh as *Al(t) Clut* (Clyde Rock), and *Din Al Clud, Caer Al Clut, Din Clut, Caer Glut,* and (in Latin) *Arx Al Clut*, all meaning 'stronghold of (the rock of) Clyde'.[7] That points to a solution for *Alutthèlia*. It is not difficult to take *Alut-* here as a corruption of *Al Clut*, an earlier form of *Alclit* (Auckland). A scribe's eye apparently skipped (owing to haplography) from the first *l* to the second, omitting *-cl-*. If so, this would explain *Al-* followed (in unusual combination for an English place name) by *-ut*. Such a copying error explains *Alut-* as *Al (Cl)ut* (Clyde Rock), or Auckland.

It makes historical as well as palaeographical sense. The Ordnance Survey *Map of Britain in the Dark Ages* shows Auckland's situation at a point where Dere Street, the Roman road from Catterick to Corbridge, crosses the River Wear. (Further north, where the highway crossed the River Browney south of Lanchester, there was to be another battle in 937, this time an English victory.) Provided with a natural stronghold on its hill, the site was of obvious strategic

---

[4] Whitelock 1979, 282.
[5] Coates and Breeze 2000, 296.
[6] Smith 1907, 70.
[7] Jackson 1969, 76.

importance. The map also records a stone Anglo-Saxon cross there (a fragment survives).[8] Auckland was clearly of significance in Anglo-Saxon times.

As for the last part of *Alutthèlia*, that can likewise be explained. It is not Celtic. It seems rather to represent a Latinization of the Old English plural *thelu* (planks), meaning a plank bridge or pathway. The form occurs elsewhere in England. It appears on modern maps at Theale 'plank bridge' in Berkshire and Somerset, as also Thelnetham (enclosure of swans by a plank bridge) in Suffolk, Thelwall (pool by a plank bridge) in Cheshire, Thelbridge (plank bridge) in Devon and Elbridge (plank bridge) in Kent, near Canterbury.[9]

On the above interpretation, then, *Alutthèlia* would be a corrupt Latinization of the *thelu* of *Al Clut* or 'plank bridge of Auckland'. The explanation appears cogent. It requires no military genius to see a bridge at Auckland as a place where King Raedwulf might try to block the advance of a Danish army. His attempt to do so ended in disaster. Therafter Northumbria was at the mercy of the Northmen.

If our reasoning is sound, it has five implications. It adds a new battle to our records, the Battle of Auckland in 844, when a Danish army massacred a Northumbrian force and slaughtered its king. It sheds light on a tragic event in Northumbria's history. Second, it provides a reference to Auckland two centuries older than any known hitherto. Third, it points to the existence of a wooden bridge across the Wear at Auckland. Archaeologists may one day find traces of this, and perhaps even of the battle and its aftermath. Fourth, it points to a task for textual scholars. If variants of *Alutthèlia* in Roger's history can be set out by those with access to the manuscripts, it may confirm (or disprove) the present hypothesis. Finally, the identification of *Alutthèlia* as Auckland Bridge, if correct, demonstrates the uses of philology (particularly Celtic philology) for historical research. It apparently solves a problem of the Anglo-Saxon and Viking past, revealing a defeat that shattered Northumbrian power, so that it was noticed by Bishop Prudentius at far-away Troyes in France.

The above was published in 2002.[10] On the slaughter at *Alutthèlia* there have since then some developments. Evidence for the form (predating by two centuries the earliest otherwise known) can now be compared with what appears on Bishop Auckland in the Cambridge dictionary.[11] As for the whole question of the Viking Conquest of Northumbria, which was so very great an event, and on which we know so little, there is now an important and

---

[8] *Map of Britain in the Dark Ages.*
[9] Mills 1991, 324.
[10] Breeze 2002a.
[11] Watts 2004, 26.

up-to-date discussion by Dr Alex Woolf of St Andrews, published five years after the appearance of the *Northern History* paper on *Alutthèlia*. He makes these points. Written sources being few, we have to turn to Northumbrian coins issued during the early ninth century, trying to deduce from them the strength of the Northumbrian economy, and the effectiveness and dating of obscure kings, together with (from the distribution of hoard-finds) the nature of Viking looting and extortion. The question of dates is especially difficult. While the Raedwulf of historical records is put in 844, the Raedwulf of the numismatists is put in about 858. In this puzzling context, Dr Woolf remarks on how 'Roger of Wendover notes the brief usurpation of Raedwulf, stating that he fought a battle against the heathens, in which he was slain, at the unidentified place *Alutthèlia*. Roger dates this episode to 844, but, if the numismatists are correct, it may have been in the later 850s.'[12]

Now, it having been shown in 2002 that *Alutthèlia* was surely Auckland Bridge, it pinpoints a location for archaeologists and others to devote their enquiries, as well as underlining the significance of Roman roads in the struggle for control of Northumbria. It may allow resolution of the dating problem. It in any case brings us nearer to Northunbria's dying agonies; where readers will now find information on the usurper Raedwulf, and the Aethelred whom he supplanted, perhaps because 'the nobles saw him as a better war-leader against Scandinavian raids', but who was succeeded again by Aethelred when Raedwulf's brief reign came to an abrupt end in (it seems) 844.[13] Such was the consequence of failure at *Alutthèlia*, the wooden bridge of Bishop Auckland.

---

[12] Woolf 2007, 70.
[13] Venning 2013, 122.

Chapter 12

893: VIKINGS LIQUIDATED AT BUTTINGTON, POWYS

The *Anglo-Saxon Chronicle* entry for 894 (*recte* 893) describes the Viking campaigns of that year. It states that 'the marauding parties were both gathered together at Shoburg [Shoebury] in Essex, and there built a fortress. Then they both went together up by the Thames, and a great concourse joined them, both from the East-Angles and from the Northumbrians. They then advanced upward by the Thames, till they arrived near the Severn. Then they proceeded upward by the Severn.' While that was happening, Alfred's generals gathered forces.

> When they were all collected together, they overtook the rear of the enemy at Buttington on the banks of the Severn, and there beset them without on each side in a fortress. When they had sat there many weeks on both sides of the river, and the king meanwhile was in Devonshire westward with the naval force, then were the enemy weighed down with famine. They had devoured the greater part of their horses; and the rest had perished with hunger. Then went they out to the men that sat on the eastern side of the river, and fought with them; but the Christians had the victory.

Notes on this translation indicate the difficulties of locating Buttington, where Viking marauders so unpleasantly starved to death. Ingram referred to John Speed (d. 1629), William Somner (d. 1669), Obadiah Walker (d. 1699) and Edward Gibson (d. 1748) for it as by Welshpool, Powys, while Sir John Spelman (d. 1643) put it in Gloucestershire. Walker actually mentioned earthworks visible at the former site (although he mistakenly placed it in Shropshire). Despite that Ingram plumped for Boddington, north-west of Cheltenham.[1] But Boddington is not on the Severn.

Later writers also show the slow progress of agreement between the seventeenth century and the twenty-first. Plummer placed the conflict at Buttington

---

[1] Ingram 1823, 117–18, 432.

Tump (National Grid Reference (NGR) ST 547931), on a peninsula between the Wye and Severn near Tiddenham, Gloucestershire.[2] Sir John Lloyd also thought Buttington by Chepstow suited the *Chronicle* account better than did Buttington by Welshpool (especially for the composition of the English army and its leaders).[3] Hugh Smith agreed, thinking 'that the two sides of the river' referred to Wye, and not to the Severn Estuary.[4] Garmonsway similarly placed Buttington in Gloucestershire.[5]

However, Mary Griffiths located the Viking camp at Buttington near Welshpool.[6] So did Dorothy Whitelock.[7] Sir Frank Stenton was decisive. Noting how the Danes moved 'up along the Severn', he came down for the northern Buttington, adding that there are traces of an island at this Buttington (NGR SJ 246087), unfortunately much changed when the railway was built.[8] In 1979 Dorothy Whitelock again referred without qualification to Buttington, Montgomeryshire.[9] Patrick Wormald (providing a helpful map) also placed the Viking fort there.[10]

Others were less confident. Keynes and Lapidge believed that the Buttington in north Powys 'seems preferable' because the Vikings 'went up along the Severn', but did not rule out the southern one.[11] Alfred Smyth, in a much-criticized volume, yet held out for the northern place, providing detailed discussion.[12] Swanton was ambiguous. He identified the Buttington of 893 as the southern one, on a 'valuable royal estate', although admitting that the northern site 'might make more sense', because Alfred's forces camped on both sides of the river. He also mentioned remains of earthworks there and a war-grave excavated in the nineteenth century.[13] So, depite Stenton's incisive argument for the northern Buttington, which were consistently supported by Dorothy Whitelock, some have still taken seriously the southern rival.

What follows is discussion of a note by Ekwall, which (despite being the longest account of the problem) has been neglected. It spotlights the pitfalls which await even the best researchers. Ekwall argued strongly for the southern

---

[2] Plummer 1899, 109–10.
[3] Lloyd 1911, 329n.32.
[4] Smith 1935, 47.
[5] Garmonsway 1953, 87.
[6] Griffiths 1962, 47.
[7] Whitelock 1967, 239.
[8] Stenton 1971, 267n.1.
[9] Whitelock 1979, 204n.1.
[10] Wormald 1982, 151.
[11] Keynes and Lapidge 1983, 287.
[12] Smyth 1995, 127.
[13] Swanton 1996, 87.

Buttington. He began by referring to Viking raids mentioned by *Annales Cambriae* and the Red Book of Hergest version of *Brut y Tywysogyon* (unaware, however, that this campaign is now dated to 896, and cannot relate to 893). He then observed how 'the long version of the *Brut* found in *Myvyrian Archaiology* on p. 688 has a much fuller account. Here we are told that in 893 the Black Heathens (the Danes) came to Wales by way of the Bristol Channel (*Mor Hafren*) and burnt Llanilltud Fawr (Llanelltud in Brecknock) [*recte*, Llantwit Major, Glamorgan]', Kenvig, Llangarfan (both in Gwent) [*recte*, Glamorgan], and did much harm in Glamorgan, Gwent (south coast), Brecknock (*Built*, Builth in Radnor?) [*recte* in north Brecknock], that on their way back to Gwynl(i)wg, while pillaging Caerleon (in Monmouthshire), they were met by Morgan, King of Glamorgan, and Cad [Ekwall wrongly takes *cad* 'battle' as a proper noun] and defeated. This must be a fuller account of the happening briefly noticed by Annales Camb. and the short version of Brut. If this account, which is not referred to Plummer, is to be trusted, and there is no reason to doubt its substantial correctness [!], it follows that the raid to South Wales was not undertaken by the Danes living at Chester, but by Danes coming by the way '*dros lyr*' over the Bristol Channel.' Ekwall concluded from this that 'it seems justifiable to identify Buttington as the one in Gloucestershire'.[14] In his *Oxford Dictionary* he steadfastly identified the Buttington of 893 as the Gloucestershire one.[15]

Ekwall quoted this 'long version of *Brut*', which gives such detailed information, from *The Myvyrian Archaiology*. He did not know that it was a forgery. It is the work of the notorious Edward Williams (1747–1826), alias 'Iolo Morganwg', a Welsh Chatterton or Macpherson. Iolo claimed that this version, 'the Aberpergwm Brut', was a twelfth-century chronicle surviving at Aberpergwm, near Neath, Glamorgan. Yet no copy of it predates two in Iolo's own hand, which are now Aberystwyth, National Library of Wales, MSS Llanover C34 and 26. Although based on the authentic 'Chronicle of the Princes', they are certainly one of Iolo's forgeries, as has long been known.[16] As evidence for the events in 893 this text is worthless. Once that is grasped, little is left of Ekwall's arguments for the southern Buttington.

We close with an account of the war grave at Buttington, Powys. In 1839 a labourer digging on the north side of the churchyard found 'about 330 human skulls deposited in three distinct holes of about a yard in diameter, and nearly a cartload of arms, legs and thighbones placed over them. The skulls were afterwards placed in the church for public inspection, and several phrenologists were of opinion that they must have been the remains of men

---

[14] Ekwall 1959, 23–25.
[15] Ekwall 1960, 79.
[16] Lewis 1971, 476.

from the age of 20 to 45, as the ossification of the cranium was of different stages.' Contemporaries soon linked these remains with the events of 893.[17] There can be no doubt that the Viking host which Alfred pursued 'after desperate battle' met its doom at Buttington, Wales.

The above was published in 2000 in a volume edited by Canon Roger Brown, of Welshpool.[18] It is encouraging to see how the case for the southern Buttington, which gained influential support in the later twentieth century, is now abandoned. It is true that no notice is taken in a standard dictionary of the 893 mention of Buttington, pre-dating the earliest given there (*Butinton*, of 1166–67) by nearly three hundred years.[19] On the other hand, Professor Charles-Edwards has no doubts on Buttington, Powys.[20] Nor does Colmán Etchingham of Maynooth, who cites Irish annals on this Viking disaster.[21] The West Saxon victory was noticed internationally. So, after four centuries, scholars can be secure on the whereabouts of one event in Britain's military history.

Buttington, with its diminutive church, is a quiet place now. But it once saw a Viking army in desperate plight, with warriors dead or dying. The siege nevertheless ended in surprise. When the survivors went forth to attack their English besiegers, they still killed many of them, and some Vikings even escaped back to Essex.

---

[17] Lewis 1844, 142.
[18] Breeze 2000.
[19] Owen and Morgan 2007, 58.
[20] Charles-Edwards 2013, 507–508.
[21] Etchingham 2014, 29, 37.

Chapter 13

937: *BRUNANBURH* AND ENGLISH TRIUMPH AT LANCHESTER, COUNTY DURHAM

At *Brunanburh*, in the late summer of 937, Athelstan of Wessex eliminated an invading army of Scots, Strathclyders and Vikings. It was a major victory, never forgotten, and crucial in uniting England, for Athelstan's success was in part due to Mercian forces under his command. But the battle's location was eventually forgotten and became a long-standing historical mystery. In 2018, however, I (following a suggestion of Alistair Campbell in 1938) published reasons to locate *Brunanburh* at the *burh* or Roman fort of Lanchester, above the *Brune* or river Browney in County Durham.[1]

That account being in book form and hence accessible to readers, there is no need to go through it again in full. All the same, for the sake of completeness, *British Battles 493–937* can be brought to an end with a chapter on it, including information on points not mentioned in the original paper.

The bibliography of *Brunanburh* is immense, like that for Mount Badon and Arthur's other Twelve Battles in *Historia Brittonum*. As with the Twelve Battles, where one finds shrewd and cogent remarks, together with a great deal of nonsense, so also with *Brunanburh*. Early scholars came close to the truth, later and lesser scholars ignore what they said.

We start with the Reverend James Ingram (1774–1850), editor and translator of the *Anglo-Saxon Chronicle*. In his edition (a handsome one, with much of interest), he could do no more than cite William Camden (1551–1623) for the suggestion of 'Bromeridge' in Northumberland, and Camden's translator Edmund Gibson (1669–1748) for Bromborough, Cheshire.[2] The latter has defenders even now. But, after three centuries, his ideas should be dismissed. The first writer to approach the correct solution seems to have been Joseph Bosworth (1789–1876). Discussing the Old English poem *The Battle of*

---

[1] Breeze 2018a.
[2] Ingram 1823, 432.

Brunanburh, he translated *Brunanburh* as 'castle of Bruna' (better, the *Brune*) and put it by the river Browney. Unfortunately, he located the battlefield not near Lanchester, but outside Durham.[3] His suggestion in any case had no influence.

The next step came in 1938, when the Oxford scholar Alistair Campbell edited *The Battle of Brunanburh*, in one of the finest ever editions of an Old English poem. He collected other names for the conflict. Besides standard ones are *Weondune* and *Wendune* in Simeon of Durham (active in about 1130), *Duinbrunde* in the so-called 'Pictish Chronicle', *Bellum Brune* in the tenth-century *Annales Cambriae* and *Plaines of othlynn* in the *Annals of Clonmacnoise*, a seventeenth-century translation of Irish annals. After extensive review of the evidence, he ended in despair, declaring that, unless new facts came to light, 'all hope of localizing Brunanburh is lost'.[4] Nevertheless, this ancillary information is significant. For all the difficulties of interpretation, it all tallies with a location on the River Browney south of Lanchester, with one exception. This is *Plaines of othlynn*, where the last word will be a corrupt rendering of Irish *otharlinn* 'pool of sickness', a rhetorical expression meaning 'place of slaughter'. Not being a toponym, it is therefore of no value on where the conflict took place.

Of sources provided by twelfth-century historians, one stands out. Simeon of Durham describes the action as 'fought at *Weondune* (which is also called *Et Brunnanwerc* or *Brunnanbyrig*) against Anlaf, the son of the former king, Guthred, who had come with six hundred and fifteen ships.'[5] There are several points of interest here. First is Simeon's precision on names. He is far more circumstantial than John of Worcester, writing at about the same time in the West Midlands. His *We(o)ndune*, which means 'round hill' (and has nothing whatever to do with the River Went of Yorkshire, discussed in Chapter 8) implies local knowledge. Because on other grounds we locate the engagement at Lanchester, it should yet be no surprise, the spot being a mere eight miles from Durham, where Simeon wrote. As for *Bellum Brune* in *Annales Cambriae*, this also gives special information, however bald and unpromising it may look. *Bellum* is medieval Latin for 'battle'. More significantly, *Brune* must be a toponym. It is not the name of some Anglo-Saxon. This can be proved by reference to the annal for 880 (in Welsh, not Latin), on *Gueit Conguoy* 'Battle of the Conway', the River Conway of North Wales.[6] The River Browney being known to the Anglo-Saxons as *Brune*, the exact preservation of this form in Celtic-Latin is confirmation for the battlefield as being near it.

---

[3] Toller 1898, 128–29.
[4] Campbell 1938, 57–80.
[5] Allen and Calder 1976, 196.
[6] Morris 1980, 48, 90.

Against this is the long-standing case, going back to Gibson in 1695, for the conflict as at Bromborough in Cheshire. Arguments of the seventeenth century were supported in the twentieth century by the respected place-name scholar John McNeal Dodgson (1928–1990), and are advanced again in the twenty-first century by Paul Cavill of Nottingham. Bromborough, which is today administratively in Merseyside, is on the north coast of the Wirral, by the Mersey Estuary. Certain difficulties are obvious from the start. There is no river or stream called 'Browney' or the like at the spot; no obvious *burh* or stronghold, in the way that there is at Lanchester, which owes its very name to such a work; and the siting on England's west coast is inconsistent with the statement by John of Worcester that Dublin-Norse allies of the Scots and Strathclyders brought their fleet in on the Humber, and so on the English east coast, there being richer pickings to be had in the former Kingdom of York than in the Lancashire-Cheshire region. There is the further point that Scots invaders of England, even as late as the Young Pretender in 1745, entered (and left) England on Roman roads (also used by English invaders of Scotland). That an army of Scots and Strathclyders should have been in the Wirral, so far from the road to the North, goes against all probability. Quite apart from the problems of shipping and logistics, a retreat into a peninsula in the face of an English army would be putting one's head into a noose. Generals know a lot about peninsulas, or should do. There are modern parallels. In 1915, British and Australasian troops landed on the Gallipoli Peninsula; despite months of fighting, they made no effective headway against the Turks (who had advance knowledge of their coming). This fiasco in mind, Allied Command in 1944 chose to make landings in central Normandy, and not in Brittany or Cotentin, even though the latter (unlike central Normandy) had ports, because the two latter were peninsulas and hence gave Germany forces better opportunities to block an advance. (The lack of a port was solved by the invention of Mulberry Harbours.) Gibson, a future Bishop of London, did not appreciate the strategic disadvantages of Bromborough from the invaders' point of view. If, instead of being a librarian and an Oxford don, he had been an army officer helping William III to defeat Louis XIV, he might have grasped the point.

There are other factors. A notorious crux occurs in lines 54–55 of *The Battle of Brunanburh*, on how the shattered Viking force fled the field, '*on Dingesmere*, / Over the deep water, Dublin to seek'. There has been an attempt to relate the baffling expression *Dingesmere* (written as one word in the manuscripts) to Thingwall in the Wirral, with the poet's phrase taken to mean 'mere of the *thing*, mere of the (Scandinavian) assembly', referring to the Irish Sea or Mersey estuary.[7] Yet it poses great difficulties of phonology and sense.

---

[7] Cavill, Harding and Jesch, 2003–2004.

Nevertheless, a study in a volume presented to Margaret Gelling correctly rules out the claims of Burnswark in south-west Scotland, and Bromswald on the Northamptonshire border.[8] It leaves open those of Bromborough, which cannot be disproved on philological grounds alone, except on one matter. There being no stream at Bromborough called 'Browney', *Brom-* is accepted as the Old English man's name *Bruna*. We do not know who Bruna was, but he certainly did not give his name to a conflict, as shown by the *Annales Cambriae* entry on *Bellum Brune* (Battle of the Brune). Engagements by land and sea and now the air (as in 1940) are called after places, not people: Blenheim, the Nile, Trafalgar, Jutland, Britain, the Atlantic. This is a further nail in the coffin for Bromborough as a meeting place of armies in the summer of 937.

In the light of these difficulties, Professor Michael Wood now tries another tack. He puts 'Wendun' on the river Went, north-west of Doncaster. He thinks 'Wendun' was near the Went, claiming that no 'pre-Conquest forms have survived' as regards the river.[9] Not so. The Went is Bede's *Uinued* '(river) of white aspect' (compare Welsh *gwyn* (white) and *gwedd* (form, appearance)), which Bede states as being in the Leeds area. The form could not have given the *Wen-* or *Weon-* supplied by Simeon of Durham, where *d* is lacking, even though it survives to this day in *Went*. A link between *Brunanburh* and the Went being out of the question on linguistic grounds, Wood's whole case collapses.

Having given these references, we look again at toponyms set out by Campbell. First, *Brunanburh*. The sense 'fort of the *Brune*, stronghold of the River Browney' should stare one in the face; and Campbell (on page 61, in note 2) actually mentions the River Browney west of Durham. Had he picked up an Ordnance Survey Map and discovered the Roman fort at Lanchester, what is argued here would have been known 80 years ago. Maps show the Roman fort of Lanchester as on a broad rounded slope (at National Grid Reference NZ 158467) with the *Brune* or Browney half a mile to the south. *Brunanburh* or *Brunnanwerc* makes sense as 'fort of the Browney, fortification of the Browney', on *Brunandune* (hill of the Browney). Situated on a main north-south Roman road, the site had obvious strategic importance. It was an exceedingly likely place for a battle of English and Scots; and all the evidence which we can find points consistently to Lanchester as where a Scots-Strathclyde-Norse army was annihilated by Athelstan. We have noticed in a previous chapter the Viking massacre of a Northumbria army at Bishop Auckland in 844; in 937, it was the turn of a Viking and Strathclyde-Scottish army to be wrecked on the same road, 11 miles further north, and in this case by united forces of

---

[8] Cavill 2008, 303–19.
[9] Wood 2013, 138–59.

Marcians and West Saxons. The fate of Anglo-Saxon kingdoms was, in part, settled by the hands of long-dead Roman engineers.

As for the sheaf of place names which fix *Brunanburh* at Lanchester, among them is Simeon of Durham's *Weondune* or *Wendun*. It has as first element Old English *wenn* (tumour), used as a hill name, as apparently with Wembury in Devon, Wendens Ambo in Essex or Great Wenham in Suffolk.[10] It well describes the round and swelling hill north of the Browney. Mutation of *e* to *-eo-*, which in Anglian is general before *u* in a following syllable (if here with intervocalic grouping of consonants), will be due to the back vowel of *dun*.[11] *Duinbrun(d)e* (fort of Browney) in the so-called 'Pictish Chronicle', with parasitic *d*, translates *Brunanburh*. *Bellum Brune* in *Annales Cambriae* keeps the form better. It is 'battle of the Browney', as already noted.

For the mysterious name *on dingesmere*, there is a simple solution, suggested by the Old English poem's 'over deep water' immediately after. We may emend to *on dingles mere* (into the sea of the dingle, onto the sea of the abyss). It will be a unique form corresponding to Middle and Modern English *dingle*. The word, uncommon in early English, is yet recorded in personal and place names, so that we can say more on it than was the case in the original article. It occurs as far north as Liverpool, with the Dingle attested as *de Dingyll* in 1246.[12] The area, rural until the 1850s or so, had a creek below a deep hollow with sandstone cliffs. The word *dingle* is especially one of the West Midlands, as indicated by field names in Cheshire, Shropshire and Worcestershire (The Dingle, Dingle Field, Dingle Piece).[13] A rare literary instance of it is in the thirteenth-century religious text *Sawles Warde*, on God's judgements as being deeper than *eni sea-dingle*. Analysis of this in a long footnote contains reference to modern English dialects, where it is recorded from the North, Worcestershire, Herefordshire, Gloucestershire and Suffolk. It also figures in West Midlands toponyms from the thirteenth century onwards. It is especially common on the Shropshire–Herefordshire border, where there are eight named 'dingles' located on the map to within seven miles of Wigmore (with its ruined castle of the Mortimers).[14]

Now, *Sawles Warde* casts light on *The Battle of Brunanburh*. With its declaration that God's judgements are 'secret, and deeper than any abyss of the sea (*then eni sea-dingle*)', it echoes Psalm 36:6 ('thy judgements are a great deep'), and was itself echoed by the young W. H. Auden, who began a poem 'Doom is dark

---

[10] Watts 2004, 661–62.

[11] Campbell 1959, 85, 88–89.

[12] Ekwall 1922, 115.

[13] Field 1972, 63.

[14] Dobson 1976, 117n3.

and deeper than any sea-dingle'.[15] He must have come across the expression in *Sawles Warde* when studying English at Oxford, when the teaching of J. R. R. Tolkien and others were making this a golden age for English historical philology. (Tolkien was brought up on the southern outskirts of Birmingham, giving him a lifelong interest in medieval West Midlands dialect.) It reveals an unexpected link between the Psalms and *The Battle of Brunanburh*, as also with English literature of the thirteenth century and the twentieth.

It also tells us something about the unknown poet of *The Battle of Brunanburh*. David Kirby noted his bookishness, on how he described the slaughter of the conflict as the greatest since the English arrived in Britain, according to 'what books tell us and our ancient sages' (there are similar phrases in Adomnán's life of Columba, Bede and *Historia Brittonum*).[16] That is the language of a priest; so, too, is citing of the Psalms. A. E. Redgate of Newcastle has even proposed, after Sarah Foot, that the poem was written by Bishop Cenwald of Worcester, an energetic prelate, who visited Germany and there left evidence for his interest in books.[17] Emended *on dingles mere* 'onto the sea of the abyss' is evidence, therefore, for the poet as both a cleric and a West Midlander. If meaningless 'on dingesmere' can be emended to *on dingles mere*, which fits the context, it not only inserts sense into where there is no-sense, but strengthens the attribution by Foot and Redgate of *The Battle of Brunanburh* to Bishop Cenwalh of Worcester. His use of the expression would betray West Midland origins. It may thus have the cheering effect of adding a new Old English poet to the canon, for *The Battle of Brunanburh* reveals a bookish knowledge of poetry that one might expect from a senior cleric, who was at the same time fulsome in praise of his sovereign, but (like Bishop Gibson over seven centuries later) had little interest in actual fighting. What is certain is that corrupt 'dinges' tells us nothing whatever about where the battle was fought. Nor, one may add, does *Plaines of othlynn*. It is no place name, but a corrupt version of Irish *otharlinn* (sick pool, lake of illness), a known rhetorical phrase for a battlefield.[18] It was perhaps corrupt in the lost Irish text used by the seventeenth-century translator.

If the above reasoning is sound, we can dismiss for ever the centuries of speculation on Brunanburh's whereabouts. We shall be confident that it took place on the Roman road by the fort of Lanchester, on hills west of Durham, where an army of Scots, Britons and Viking Irish was massacred (albeit with heavy English losses) in the August or September of 937. It was a famous victory, recalled in Old English sermons, Old Norse saga and even Welsh

---

[15] Bennett 1986, 280.
[16] Kirby 1996, 1.
[17] Redgate 2014, 87.
[18] *Dictionary of the Irish Language* 1913–76, letter O, column 168.

poetry.[19] Another and special monument to it is a copy of Latin lives of St Cuthbert, now Cambridge, Corpus Christi College, MS 183, with a well-known representation of Athelstan bowing to Cuthbert as the king presents a book to the saint. It seems that the manuscript was written in Wessex as Athelstan's personal gift to the monks of Chester-le-Street, handed over in the celebrations of his triumph over foreign invaders; the volume eventually moving (with its community) to Durham and, after the Dissolution of the Monasteries, ending up in Cambridge.[20]

This and other evidence placing *Brunanburh* firmly in the English north-east can now be studied at length. It allow everyone, especially people of the North who take pride in their history, to decide whether this 'Hastings of the Tenth Century' was fought there, or whether (as some still think) it took place at Bromborough, Merseyside.[21] Other opinions will also look strange in the light of what is set out above. An instance can be given already. In a volume that came to hand after this chapter was written, a professor of history at Swansea University opines that Hywel Dda (d. 949/50) did not 'assist his English allies against his own countrymen, particularly in the major uprising of 937 against King Athelstan that culminated in the Battle of *Brunanburh*'. To this she adds a comment on *Armes Prydein* (The Prophecy of Britain) as a poem of 'around 930' calling for war on the English.[22] There are various misconceptions here. The events of 937 were not an 'uprising' but a foreign invasion. Nor were the Britons of Strathclyde who invaded northern England, in the company of Scots and Dublin-Norse, the 'countrymen' of Hywel. As for *Armes Prydein*, a ferocious denunciation of the English, it dates not from 'around 930' but to the later months of 940, and so after *Brunanburh*. Its scornful references to *Lego* and *Arlego* are to *Legorensis civitas* or Leicester, where Athelstan's successor Edmund (d. 946) made a humiliating capitulation to the Vikings in 940, so that an unknown Welsh bard saw England's difficulty as Wales's opportunity.[23]

In short, although the political documents of this period can now be given proper dating, and the places in them given proper location, it will be a while before this is understood as it should be. When that is done, it will be seen that they make sense in the context of tenth-century Britain, as they do not in most present-day interpretations.

---

[19] Breeze 1993.
[20] Breeze 2016a.
[21] Clarkson 2018, 102.
[22] Skinner 2018, 7.
[23] Breeze 1997.

BIBLIOGRAPHY

Alcock, Leslie, 1971, *Arthur's Britain*. London: Allen Lane.

———, 1972, *'By South Cadbury Is That Camelot': Excavations at Cadbury Castle 1966-70*. London: Thames and Hudson.

———, 1995, *Cadbury Castle, Somerset*. Cardiff: University of Wales Press.

Allen, M. J. B., and Calder, D. G., 1976, *Sources and Analogues of Old English Poetry*. Cambridge: D. S. Brewer.

Anderson, A. O., 1908, *Scottish Annals from English Chroniclers*. London: David Nutt.

Anderson. M. O., 1973, *Kings and Kingship in Early Scotland*. Edinburgh: Scottish Academic Press.

Aurell, Martin, 2007, *La Légende du roi Arthur*. Paris: Perrin.

Bannerman, John, 1968, 'The Dál Riata and Northern Ireland', in James Carney and David Greene (eds), *Celtic Studies*, 1–11. New York: Barnes and Noble.

———, 1974, *Studies in the History of Dalriada*. Edinburgh: Scottish Academic Press.

Bartrum, P. C., 1966, *Early Welsh Genealogical Tracts*. Cardiff: University of Wales Press.

Bennett, J. A. W., 1986, *Middle English Literature*. Oxford: Clarendon.

Blockley, Kevin, 1990, 'Excavations in the Vicinity of Forden Gaer Roman Fort, Powys, 1987', *Mongomeryshire Collections* 78, 17–46.

Bollard, John, 2019, 'The Earliest Myrddin Poems', in Ceridwen Lloyd-Morgan and Erich Poppe (eds), *Arthur in the Celtic Languages*, 35–50. Cardiff: University of Wales Press.

Breeze, A., 1993, 'The Battle of Brunanburh and Welsh Tradition', *Neophilologus* 83, 479–82.

———, 1997, *'Armes Prydein*, Hywel Dda, and the Reign of Edmund of Wessex', *Études celtiques* 33, 209–22.

———, 2000, 'The *Anglo-Saxon Chronicle* for 893 and Buttington', in R. L. Brown (ed.), *The Sayce Papers: Sword and Money*, 47–50. Welshpool: Gwasg Eglwys y Trallwng.

———, 2001, 'Seventh-Century Northumbria and a Poem to Cadwallon', *Northern History* 38, 145–52.

———, 2002a, 'The Battle of *Alutthèlia* in 844 and Bishop Auckland', *Northern History* 39, 124–25.

———, 2002b, 'The Kingdom and Name of Elmet', *Northern History* 39, 157–71.

———, 2004, 'The Battle of the *Uinued* and the River Went, Yorkshire', *Northern History* 41, 377–83.

———, 2007, 'Bede's *Hefenfeld* and the Campaign of 633', *Northern History* 44, 193–97.

———, 2009, *The Origins of the 'Four Branches of the Mabinogi'*. Leominster: Gracewing.

———, 2012a, 'The Name and Battle of Arfderydd, Near Carlisle', *Journal of Literary Onomastics* 2, 1–9.

———, 2012b, 'Did a Woman Write the Whitby Life of St Gregory?', *Northern History* 49, 345–50.

————, 2013, '613: The Battle of Chester and "King Cetula"', *Northern History* 50, 115–19.

————, 2014, '633 and the Battle of Hatfield Chase', *Northern History* 51, 177–82.

————, 2015a, 'The Arthurian Battle of Badon and Braydon Forest, Wiltshire', *Journal of Literary Onomastics* 4, 20–30.

————, 2015b, 'Urien Rheged and Battle at Gwen Ystrad', *Northern History* 52, 9–19.

————, 2015c, 'The Historical Arthur and Sixth-Century Scotland', *Northern History* 52, 158–81.

————, 2016a, 'The Battle of Brunanburh and Cambridge, CCC, MS 183', *Northern History* 53, 138–45.

————, 2016b, 'Arthur's Battles and the Volcanic Winter of 536–537', *Northern History* 53, 161–72.

————, 2018a, '*Brunanburh* Located: The Battlefield and the Poem', in Michiko Ogura and Hans Sauer (eds), *Aspects of Medieval English Language and Literature*, 61–80. Berlin: Peter Lang.

————, 2018b, 'The Wharfe and *Verbeia*, Celtic Goddess', *Revue de Traduction et Langues* 17/1, 7–18.

————, 2018c, 'Lancashire and the British Kingdom of Rheged', *Transactions of the Historic Society of Lancashire and Cheshire* 167, 1–19.

Bromwich, Rachel, 1954, 'The Character of the Early Welsh Tradition', in N. K. Chadwick (ed.), *Studies in Early British History*, 83–136. Cambridge: Cambridge University Press.

————, 1978a, 'Rhagymadrodd', in Rachel Bromwich and R. Brinley Jones (eds), *Astudiaethau ar yr Hengerdd*, 1–24. Caerdydd: Gwasg Prifysgol Cymru.

———— (ed.), 1978b, *Trioedd Ynys Prydein*, 2nd edn. Cardiff: University of Wales Press.

Bromwich, Rachel, and Evans, D. Simon (eds), 1992, *Culhwch and Olwen*. Cardiff: University of Wales Press.

Byrne, F. J., 1973, *Irish Kings and High-Kings*. London: Batsford.

Campbell, A. (ed.), 1938, *The Battle of Brunanburh*. London: Heinemann.

————, 1959, *Old English Grammar*. Oxford: Clarendon.

Campbell, James, 1982a, 'The Lost Centuries', in James Campbell (ed.), *The Anglo-Saxons*, 20–44. Oxford: Phaidon.

————, 1982b, 'The First Christian Kings', in James Campbell (ed.), *The Anglo-Saxons*, 45–69. Oxford: Phaidon.

————, 2010, 'Secular and Political Contexts', in Scott DeGregorio (ed.), *The Cambridge Companion to Bede*, 25–39. Cambridge: Cambridge University Press.

Carrera, A., and Carrera, M. J. (eds), 2009, *Philip Perry's Sketch of the Ancient British History*. Newcastle upon Tyne: Cambridge Scholars.

Carver, Martin, 1998, *Sutton Hoo*. London: British Museum.

Cavill, P., 2008, 'The Site of the Battle of Brunanburh', in O. J. Padel and D. N. Parsons (eds), *A Commodity of Good Names*, 303–19. Donington: Shaun Tyas.

Cavill, P., Harding, S., and Jesch, J., 2003–2004, 'Revisiting *Dingesmere*', *Journal of the English Place-Name Society* 36, 25–38.

Chadwick, H. M., 1954, 'Vortigern', in N. K. Chadwick (ed.), *Studies in Early British History*, 21–43. Cambridge: Cambridge University Press.

Chadwick, H. M., and Chadwick, N. K., 1932, *The Growth of Literature: The Ancient Literatures of Europe*. Cambridge: Cambridge University Press.

Chadwick, N. K., 1958, 'Early Culture and Learning in North Wales', in N. K. Chadwick (ed.). *Studies in the Early British Church*, 29–120. Cambridge: Cambridge University Press.

——, 1963, 'The Battle of Chester', in N. K. Chadwick (ed.), *Celt and Saxon*, 167–85. Cambridge: Cambridge University Press.

Chambers, E. K., 1927, *Arthur of Britain*. London: Sidgwick and Jackson.

Charles, B. G., 1963, 'The Welsh, Their Language and Place-Names in Archenfield and Oswestry', in Anon. (ed.), *Angles and Britons*, 85–110. Cardiff: University of Wales Press.

Charles-Edwards, T. M., 2001, 'Wales and Mercia, 613–918', in Michelle Brown and Carol Farr (eds), *Mercia: An Anglo-Saxon Kingdom in Europe*, 89–105. London: Leicester University Press.

——, 2013, *Wales and the Britons 350–1064*. Oxford: Oxford University Press.

Churchill, W. S., 1956, *A History of the English-Speaking Peoples: The Birth of Britain*. London: Cassell.

Clancy, J. P., 1970, *The Earliest Welsh Poetry*. London: Macmillan.

Clancy, T. O., 2013, 'The Kingdoms of the North: Poetry, Places, Politics', in Alex Woolf (ed.), *Beyond the Gododdin*, 153–75. St Andrews: University of St Andrews.

Clark, Felicity, 2011, 'Thinking about Western Northumbria', in David Petts and Sam Turner (eds), *Early Medieval Northumbria*, 113–28. Turnhout: Brepols.

Clarke, Basil (ed.), 1973, *Life of Merlin*. Cardiff: University of Wales Press.

Clarke, Catherine A. M., 2006, *Literary Landscapes and the Idea of England 700–1400*. Cambridge: D. S. Brewer.

Clarkson, Tim, 2010, *The Men of the North*. Edinburgh: John Donald.

——, 2014, *Strathclyde and the Anglo-Saxons in the Viking Age*. Edinburgh: John Donald.

——, 2016, *Scotland's Merlin*. Edinburgh: John Donald.

——, 2018, *Æthelflaed: The Lady of the Mercians*. Edinburgh: John Donald.

Clayton, P. A., 1980, 'Gazetteer', in P. A. Clayton (ed.), *A Companion to Roman Britain*, 153–97. Oxford: Phaidon.

Coates, R., and Breeze, A., 2000, *Celtic Voices, English Places*. Stamford: Shaun Tyas.

Colgrave, B., and Mynors, R. A. B. (eds), 1969, *Bede's Ecclesiastical History of the English People*. Oxford: Clarendon.

Collingwood, R. G., and Myres, J. N. L., 1937, *Roman Britain and the English Settlements*, 2nd edn. Oxford: Clarendon.

Crépin, André, and Lapidge, Michael (eds), 2005a, *Histoire ecclésiastique du peuple anglais: Tome I*. Paris: Cerf.

——, (eds), 2005b, *Histoire ecclésiastique du peuple anglais: Tome II*. Paris: Cerf.

Cullen, Paul, 2008, 'The Survival of a British Place-Name in Kent', in O. J. Padel and D. N. Parsons (eds), *A Commodity of Good Names*, 95–100. Stamford: Shaun Tyas.

Daniel, Catherine, 2006, *Les prophéties de Merlin et la culture politique*. Turnhout: Brepols.

Daniel, Iestyn (ed.), 2019, *Llythyr Gildas a Dinistr Prydain*. Bangor: Dalen Newydd.

Dark, K. R., 1994, *Civitas to Kingdom*. London: Leicester University Press.

——, 2000, 'A Famous Arthur in the Sixth Century?', *Reading Medieval Studies* 26, 77–95.

Davies, Ceri, 1995, *Wales and the Classical Tradition*. Cardiff: University of Wales Press.

Davies, Pennar, 1966, *Rhwng Chwedl a Chredo*. Caerdydd: Gwasg Prifysgol Cymru.

Davies, Wendy, 1982, *Wales in the Early Middle Ages*. Leicester: Leicester University Press.

——, 1979, *The Llandaff Charters*. Aberystwyth: National Library of Wales.

Denholm-Young, Noël, 1964, *Handwriting in England and Wales*, 2nd edn. Cardiff: University of Wales Press.

Dickins, Bruce, 1963, '"Dewi Sant" (St David) in Early English Kalendars and Place-Names', in N. K. Chadwick (ed.), *Celt and Saxon*, 206–209. Cambridge: Cambridge University Press.

Dictionary of the Irish Language, 1913–76. Dublin: Royal Irish Academy.

Dickinson, W. Croft, 1977, *Scotland from the Earliest Times to 1603*, 2nd edn. Oxford: Clarendon.

Doble, G. H., 1971, *Lives of the Welsh Saints*. Cardiff: University of Wales Press.

Dobson, E. J., 1976, *The Origins of 'Ancrene Wisse'*, Oxford: Clarendon.

Draper, S., 2011, 'Towards an Archaeological Interpretation of Place-Names in Wiltshire', in N. J. Higham and M. J. Ryan (eds), *Place-Names, Language, and the Anglo-Saxon Landscape*, 85–104. Woodbridge: Boydell.

Dumville, D. N., 1977, 'Sub-Roman Britain: History and Legend', *History* 72, 173–92.

——, 1984, 'Gildas and Maelgwn: Problems of Dating', in Michael Lapidge and David Dumville (eds), *Gildas: New Approaches*, 51–59. Woodbridge: Boydell.

——, 1988, 'Early Welsh Poetry: Problems of Historicity', in B. F. Roberts (ed.) *Early Welsh Poetry*, 1–16. Aberystwyth: National Library of Wales.

—— (ed.), 2002, *Annales Cambriae AD 682–984*. Cambridge: Department of Anglo-Saxon, Norse and Celtic.

—— (ed.), 2005, *Brenhinoedd y Saeson*. Aberdeen: Department of History.

——, 2011, 'Political Organization in Dál Riata', in Fiona Edmonds and Paul Russell (ed.), *Tome*, 41–52. Woodbridge: Boydell.

Duncan, A. A. M., 1975, *Scotland: The Making of the Kingdom*. Edinburgh: Oliver and Boyd.

——, 1981, 'Bede, Iona, and the Picts', in R. H. C. Davis and J. M. Wallace-Hadrill (eds), *The Writing of History in the Middle Ages*, 1–42. Oxford: Clarendon.

Edmonds, Fiona, 2011, *Whithorn's Renown in the Early Medieval Period*. Whithorn: Friends of the Whithorn Trust.

Edwards, Charles, 1948, *Hanes y Ffydd yng Nghymru*. Caerdydd: Gwasg Prifysgol Cymru.

Edwards, Nancy, 2013, *A Corpus of Early Medieval Inscribed Stones and Stone Sculpture from Wales: North Wales*. Cardiff: University Wales Press.

——, 2017, 'Chi-Rhos, Crosses, and Pictish Symbols', in Nancy Edwards, Máire Ní Mhaonaigh and Roy Fletchner (eds), *Transforming Landscapes of Belief in the Early Medieval Insular World and Beyond: Converting the Isles II*, 381–407. Turnhout: Brepols.

Ekwall, Eilert, 1922, *The Place-Names of Lancashire*. Manchester: Manchester University Press.

——, 1936, *The Concise Oxford Dictionary of English Place-Names*. Oxford: Clarendon.

——, 1959, *Etymological Notes and English Place-Names*. Lund: Gleerup.

——, 1960, *The Concise Oxford Dictionary of English Place-Names*, 4th edn. Oxford: Clarendon.

Etchingham, Colmán, 2014, 'Names for the Vikings in Irish Annals', in J. V. Sigurðsson and Timothy Bolton (eds), *Celtic-Norse Relations in the Irish Sea in the Middle Ages 800–1200*, 23–38. Leiden: Brill.

Evans, Dai Morgan, 2006, ' "King Arthur" and Cadbury Castle, Somerset', *The Antiquaries Journal* 86, 226–53.

Evans, D. Simon (ed.), 1977, *Historia Gruffud vab Kenan*. Caerdydd: Gwasg Prifysgol Cymru.

——, 1988, *The Welsh Life of St David*. Cardiff: University of Wales Press.

Evans, Geraint, and Fulton, Helen (eds), 2019, *The Cambridge History of Welsh Literature*. Cambridge: Cambridge University Press.

Evans, J. Gwenogvryn (ed.), 1893, *The Text of the Book of Llan Dâv*. Oxford: Privately printed.

——, (ed.) 1910, *The Text of the Book of Taliesin*. Llanbedrog: Privately printed.

Evans, Theophilus, 1961, *Drych y Prif Oesoedd*. Caerdydd: Gwasg Prifysgol Cymru.

Falileyev, A., 2010, *Dictionary of Continental Celtic Place-Names*. Aberystwyth: Cambrian Medieval Celtic Studies.

Favero, Piero, 2012, *La dea veneta: Dal Baltico alla Bretagna*, 2nd edn. Verona: Cierre Grafica.

Field, John, 1972, *English Field-Names*. Newton Abbot: David and Charles.

Finberg, H. P. R., 1972, 'Anglo-Saxon England', in H. P. R. Finberg (ed.), *The Agrarian History of England and Wales: AD 43–1042*, 383–532. Cambridge: Cambridge University Press.

———, 1974. *The Formation of England.* London: Hart-Davis.

Förster, Max, 1941, *Der Flussname Themse und seine Sippe.* München: Bayerische Akademie der Wissenschaften.

Forsyth, Katherine, 2009, 'The Latinus Stone', in Jane Murray (ed.), *St Ninian and the Earliest Christianity in Scotland,* 19–41. Oxford: Archaeopress.

Foster, I. Ll., 1965, 'The Emergence of Wales', in I. Ll. Foster and Glyn Daniel (eds), *Prehistoric and Early Wales,* 213–35. London: Routledge.

Fraser, J. E., 2009, *From Caledonia to Pictland: Scotland to 795.* Edinburgh: Edinburgh University Press.

Frere, S. S., 1967, *Britannia.* London: Routledge.

Garmonsway, G. N. (tr.), 1953, *The Anglo-Saxon Chronicle.* London: Dent.

Geiriadur Prifysgol Cymru, 1950–2002. Caerdydd: Gwasg Prifysgol Cymru.

Gelling, Margaret, 1970, 'Oswestry', in W. F. H. Nicolaisen (ed.), *The Names of Towns and Cities in Britain,* 146–47. London: Batsford.

———, 1978, *Signposts to the Past.* London: Dent.

———, 1984, *Place-Names in the Landscape.* London: Dent.

George, Karen, 2009, *Gildas's 'De Excidio Britonum' and the Early British Church.* Woodbridge: Boydell.

Gibbon, Edward, 1904, *The History of the Decline and Fall of the Roman Empire, IV.* London: Oxford University Press.

Gillingham, John, 2015, 'Richard of Devizes and "A Rising Tide of Nonsense"', in Martin Brett and D. A. Woodman (eds), *The Long Twelfth-Century View of the Anglo-Saxon Past,* 141–56. Farnham: Ashgate.

Griffiths, M. E., 1962, 'King Alfred's Last War', in Norman Davies and C. L. Wrenn (eds), *English and Medieval Studies Presented to J. R. R. Tolkien.* London: Allen and Unwin.

Gruffydd, R. G., 1978, 'Canu Cadwallon ap Cadfan', in Rachel Bromwich and R. Brinley Jones (eds), *Astudiaethau ar yr Hengerdd,* 25–43. Caerdydd: Gwasg Prifysgol Cymru.

———, 1982, 'Marwnad Cynddylan', in R. G. Gruffydd (ed.), *Bardos,* 10–28. Caerdydd: Gwasg Prifysgol Cymru.

———, 2002, *'Edmyg Dinbych'.* Aberystwyth: Canolfan Uwchefrydiadau.

Haddan, A. W., and Stubbs, W., 1869–78, *Councils and Ecclesiastical Documents Relating to Great Britain and Ireland.* Oxford: Clarendon.

Halsall, Guy, 2013, *Worlds of Arthur.* Oxford: Oxford University Press.

Hanson, R. P. C., 1968, *Saint Patrick.* Oxford: Clarendon.

Harris, Silas M., 1940, *Saint David in the Liturgy.* Cardiff: University of Wales Press.

Haslam, Richard, 1978, *The Buildings of Wales: Powys.* Harmondsworth: Penguin.

Haycock, Marged (ed.), 2007, *Legendary Poems from the Book of Taliesin.* Aberystwyth: Cambrian Medieval Celtic Studies.

——— (ed.), 2013, 'Early Welsh Poets Look North', in Alex Woolf (ed.), *Beyond the Gododdin,* 7–39. St Andrews: University of St Andrews.

Henderson, Isabel, 1967, *The Picts.* London: Thames and Hudson.

Higham, N. J., 1993, *The Origins of Cheshire.* Manchester: Manchester University Press.

———, 1995, *An English Empire.* Manchester: Manchester University Press.

———, 2001, 'Britons in Northern England in the Early Middle Ages', *Northern History* 38, 5–25.

———, 2002, *King Arthur: Myth-Making and History.* London: Routledge.

———, 2006, *(Re-)Reading Bede.* Manchester: Manchester University Press.

————, 2011, 'The Chroniclers of Early Britain', in Siân Echard (ed.), *The Arthur of Medieval Latin Literature*, 9–25. Cardiff: University of Wales Press.

————, 2018, *King Arthur: The Making of the Legend*. New Haven: Yale University Press.

Hill, David, 1981, *An Atlas of Anglo-Saxon England*. Oxford: Blackwell.

Holthausen, F., 1932–34, *Altenglisches etymologisches Wörterbuch*. Heidelberg: Winter.

Houlder, Christopher, 1974, *Wales: An Archaeological Guide*. London: Faber.

Hunter Blair, Peter, 1954, 'The Bernicians and Their Northern Frontier', in N. K. Chadwick (ed.), *Studies in Early British History*, 137–72. Cambridge: Cambridge University Press.

————, 1963, *Roman Britain and Early England*. Edinburgh: Nelson.

————, 1970, *The Age of Bede*. London: Secker and Warburg.

————, 1976, *Northumbria in the Days of Bede*. London: Gollancz.

————, 1977, *An Introduction to Anglo-Saxon England*, 2nd edn. Cambridge: Cambridge University Press.

Ingram, James (ed.), 1823, *The Saxon Chronicle*. London: Longman.

Ireland, S., 1996, *Roman Britain: A Sourcebook*. London: Routledge.

Isaac, G. R., 1998, '*Gwaith Gwen Ystrat* and the Northern Heroic Age', *Cambrian Medieval Celtic Studies* 36, 61–70.

Jackson, K. H., 1953, *Language and History in Early Britain*. Edinburgh: Edinburgh University Press.

————, 1955, 'The Britons in Southern Scotland', *Antiquity* 19, 77–88.

————, 1958, 'The Sources for the Life of St Kentigern', in N. K. Chadwick (ed.), *Studies in the Early British Church*, 273–357. Cambridge: Cambridge University Press.

————, 1959a, 'The Arthur of History', in R. S. Loomis (ed.), *Arthurian Literature in the Middle Ages*, 1–11. Oxford: Clarendon.

————, 1959b, 'Edinburgh and the Anglian Occupation of Lothian', in Peter Clemoes (ed.), *The Anglo-Saxons*, 35–42. London: Bowes and Bowes.

————, 1963a, 'Angles and Britons in Northumbria and Cumbria', in Anon. (ed.), *Angles and Britons*, 60–84. Cardiff: University of Wales Press.

————, 1963b, 'On the Northern British Section in Nennius', in N. K. Chadwick (ed.), *Celt and Saxon*, 20–62. Cambridge: Cambridge University Press.

————, 1969, *The Gododdin: The Oldest Scottish Poem*. Edinburgh: Edinburgh University Press.

————, 1977, ' "O Achaws Nyth yr Ychedydd" ', *Ysgrifau Beiniadol* 10, 45–50.

Jankulak, Karen, 2010, *Writers of Wales: Geoffrey of Monmouth*. Cardiff: University of Wales Press.

Jarman, A. O. H., 1959, 'The Welsh Myrddin Poems', in R. S. Loomis (ed.), *Arthurian Literature in the Middle Ages*, 20–30. Oxford: Clarendon.

————, 1960, *The Legend of Merlin*. Cardiff: University of Wales Press.

———— (ed.), 1967, *Ymddiddan Myrddin a Thaliesin*, 2nd edn. Caerdydd: Gwasg Prifysgol Cymru.

————, 1978, 'Early Stages in the Development of the Myrddin Legend', in Rachel Bromwich and R. Brinley Jones (eds), *Astudiaethau ar yr Hengerdd*, 326–49. Cardiff: University of Wales Press.

————, 2003, 'The Merlin Legend and the Welsh Tradition of Prophecy', in P. H. Goodrich and R. H. Thompson (eds), *Merlin: A Casebook*, 105–30. New York: Routledge.

Johnson, Flint F., 2014, *Evidence of Arthur*. Jefferson: McFarland.

Johnson, Stephen, 1980, *Later Roman Britain*. London: Routledge.

Jones, G. R. J., 1972, 'Post-Roman Wales', in H. P. R. Finberg (ed.), *The Agrarian History of England and Wales: AD 43–1042*, 279–382. Cambridge: Cambridge University Press.

Jones, Nerys Anne, 2019, 'Arthurian References in Early Welsh Poetry', in Ceridwen Lloyd-Morgan and Erich Poppe (eds), *Arthur in the Celtic Languages*, 15–34. Cardiff: University of Wales Press.

Jones, Nerys Anne, and Owen, Ann Parry (eds), 1991–95, *Gwaith Cynddelw Brydydd Mawr*. Caerdydd: Gwasg Prifysgol Cymru.

Jones, Owen, Williams, Edward, and Pughe, W. O. (eds), 1870, *The Myvyrian Archaiology of Wales*, 2nd edn. Denbigh: Gee.

Kennedy, E. D., 2010, 'Historia Brittonum', in Graeme Dunphy (ed.), *The Encyclopedia of the Medieval Chronicle*, 790–91. Leiden: Brill.

Keynes, S. D., and Lapidge, M., 1983, *The Age of Alfred*. Harmondsworth: Penguin.

Kirby, D. P., 1967, *The Making of Early England*. London: Batsford.

———, 1996, *History and Tradition in Britain in the Early Middle Ages*. Aberystwyth: University of Wales.

Kłos, Jan, 2017, *Kryzys cywilizacji europejskiej wobec chrześcijaństwa w myśli Juana Donoso Cortésa*. Lublin: Wydawnictwo Academicon.

Koch, J. T., 2007, *An Atlas for Celtic Studies*. Oxford: Oxpens.

———, 2013, ' "Waiting for Gododdin" ', in Alex Woolf (ed.), *Beyond the Gododdin*, 177–204. St Andrews: University of St Andrews.

Lapidge, M., 2014. 'Gildas Sapiens', in Michael Lapidge and Francesco Santi (eds), *Compendium Auctorum Latinorum Medii Aevii: Galterius de Argentina – Guillelmus de Congenis*, 362–63. Firenze: Galluzzo.

Leland, J., 1774, *De Rebus Britannicis Collectanea*, 2nd edn. Londini: Benjamin White.

Levison, Wilhelm, 1946, *England and the Continent in the Eighth Century*. Oxford: Clarendon.

Lewis, C. P., 2007, 'Welsh Territories and Welsh Identities in Late Anglo-Saxon England', in N. J. Higham (ed.), *Britons in Anglo-Saxon England*, 130–43. Woodbridge: Boydell.

Lewis, C. W., 1971, 'The Literary Tradition of Morgannwg', in T. B. Pugh (ed.), *Glamorgan County History: The Middle Ages*, 449–554. Cardiff: Glamorgan County History Committee.

Lewis, Henry (ed.), 1931, *Hen Gerddi Crefyddol*. Caerdydd: Gwasg Prifysgol Cymru.

——— (ed.), 1942, *Brut Dingestow*. Caerdydd: Gwasg Prifysgol Cymru.

Lewis, Samuel, 1844, *A Topographical Dictionary of Wales*, 3rd edn. London: S. Lewis.

Liebhard, Kurt, 2016, *Suche nach dem historischen Arthur*. Weissenthurm: Cardamina.

Lloyd, J. E., 1911, *A History of Wales*. London: Longmans.

Lloyd-Jones, John, 1931–63, *Geirfa Barddoniaeth Gynnar Gymraeg*. Caerdydd: Gwasg Prifysgol Cymru.

Lloyd-Morgan, Ceridwen, and Poppe, Erich, 2019, 'Introduction', in Ceridwen Lloyd-Morgan and Erich Poppe (eds), *Arthur in the Celtic Languages*, 1–10. Cardiff: University of Wales Press.

Loyn, H. R., 1962, *Anglo-Saxon England and the Norman Conquest*. London: Longman.

———, 1984a, *The Governance of Anglo-Saxon England*. London: Arnold.

———, 1984b, 'The Conversion of the English to Christianity', in R. R. Davies, R. A. Griffiths, I. G. Jones and K. O. Morgan (eds), *Welsh Society and Nationhood*, 5–18. Cardiff: University of Wales Press.

Mac Cana, Proinsias, 2007, 'Ireland and Wales in the Middle Ages: An Overview', in Karen Jankulak and J. M. Wooding (eds), *Ireland and Wales in the Middle Ages*, 17–45. Dublin: Four Courts.

Mac Niocaill, Gearóid, 1972, *Ireland before the Vikings*. Dublin: Gill and Macmillan.

Map of Britain in the Dark Ages, 2nd edn, 1966. Southampton: Ordnance Survey.

Map of Roman Britain, 3rd edn, 1956. Chessington: Ordnance Survey.

Margary, I. D., 1955–57, *Roman Roads in Britain*. London: Routledge.

Mayr-Harting, H. M., 1972, *The Coming of Christianity to Anglo-Saxon England*. London: Batsford.

McCarthy, Mike, 2011, 'The Kingdom of Rheged: A Landscape Perspective', *Northern History* 48, 9–22.

McKenna, Catherine A. (ed.), 1991, *The Medieval Welsh Religious Lyric*. Belmont: Ford and Bailie.

Miller, Molly, 1975, 'The Commanders at Arthuret', *Transactions of the Cumberland and Westmorland Antiquarian and Archaeological Society* 75, 96–118.

Mills, A. D., 1991, *A Dictionary of English Place-Names*. Oxford: Oxford University Press.

Moody, T. W., Martin, F. X., and Byrne, F. J. (eds), 1982, *A New History of Ireland: A Chronology of Irish History to 1976*. Oxford: Clarendon.

Morgan, Gerald, 2015, 'The Early Welsh Cult of Arthur', *Res Celticae* 1, 133–35.

Morgan, Richard, 2008, 'Place-Names in the Northern Marches of Wales', in O. J. Padel and D. N. Parsons (eds), *A Commodity of Good Names*, 204–16. Stamford: Shaun Tyas.

Morris, John, 1973, *The Age of Arthur*. London: Weidenfeld.

——— (ed.), 1980, *British History and the Welsh Annals*. Chichester: Phillimore.

———, 1982, *Londinium*. London: Weidenfeld.

Myres, J. N. L., 1986, *The English Settlements*. Oxford: Oxford University Press.

Needham, G. I. (ed.), 1966, *Lives of Three English Saints*. London: Methuen.

Nicolaisen, W. F. H., 2002, *Scottish Place-Names*, 2nd edn. Edinburgh: John Donald.

Owen, H. W., and Morgan, R., 2007, *Dictionary of the Place-Names of Wales*. Llandysul: Gomer.

Padel, O. J., 1988, *A Popular Dictionary of Cornish Place-Names*. Penzance: Alison Hodge.

———, 1994, 'The Nature of Arthur', *Cambrian Medieval Celtic Studies* 27, 1–31.

———, 1999, 'Arthur', in Michael Lapidge, John Blair, Simon Keynes and Donald Scragg (eds), *The Blackwell Encyclopedia of Anglo-Saxon England*, 48. Oxford: Blackwell.

———, 2000, *Writers of Wales: Arthur in Medieval Welsh Literature*. Cardiff: University of Wales Press.

———, 2013, *Writers of Wales: Arthur in Medieval Welsh Literature*, rev. edn. Cardiff: University of Wales Press.

Parry, Thomas (ed.), 1952, *Gwaith Dafydd ap Gwilym*. Caerdydd: Gwasg Prifysgol Cymru.

———, 1955, *A History of Welsh Literature*. Oxford: Clarendon.

Peeblesshire: An Inventory of the Ancient Monuments, 1967. Edinburgh: Her Majesty's Stationery Office.

Plummer, C. (ed.), 1896, *Venerabilis Baedae Historia Ecclesiastica*. Oxonii: E Typographeo Clarendoniano.

——— (ed.), 1899, *Two of the Saxon Chronicles Parallel: Introduction, Notes, and Index*. Oxford: Clarendon.

———, 1925, *Miscellanea Hagiographica Hibernica*. Bruxelles: Société des Bollandistes.

Rahtz, Philip, 1976, 'Buildings and Rural Settlement', in D. M. Wilson (ed.), *The Archaeology of Anglo-Saxon England*, 49–98. Cambridge: Cambridge University Press.

Redgate, A. E., 2014, *Religion, Politics, and Society in Britain 800–1066*. London: Routledge.

Rees, R. R., 2000, *The First English Empire*. Oxford: Oxford University Press.

Rees, William, 1951, *An Historical Atlas of Wales*. London: Faber.

Rhys, John, 1904, *Celtic Britain*, 3rd edn. London: Society for Promoting Christian Knowledge.

Richards, Melville (ed.), 1948, *Breudwyt Ronabwy*. Caerdydd: Gwasg Prifysgol Cymru.

Rivet, A. L. F., and Smith, C., 1979, *The Place-Names of Roman Britain*. Princeton: Princeton University Press.

Roberts, Enid, 1965, *Braslun o Hanes Llên Powys*. Dinbych: Gee.

Rowland, Jenny, 1990, *Early Welsh Saga Poetry*. Cambridge: D. S. Brewer.

Salway, Peter, 1981, *Roman Britain*. Oxford: Oxford University Press.

Sawyer, P. H., 1978, *From Roman Britain to Norman England*. London: Methuen.

Schustereder, S., 2015, *Strategies of Identity Construction: The Writings of Gildas, Aneirin, and Bede*. Göttingen: Vandenhoeck & Ruprecht.

Sherley-Price, Leo (tr.), 1968, *A History of the English Church and People*. Harmondsworth: Penguin.

Sims-Williams, Patrick, 1984, 'Gildas and Vernacular Poetry', in Michael Lapidge and David Dumville (eds), *Gildas: New Approaches*, 169–92. Woodbridge: Boydell.

———, 2011, *Irish Influence on Medieval Welsh Literature*. Oxford: Oxford University Press.

———, 2016, 'Dating the Poems of Aneirin and Taliesin', *Zeitschrift für celtische Philologie* 63, 163–234.

Skinner, Patricia, 2018, 'Welsh Diaspora History', in Patricia Skinner (ed.), *The Welsh and the Medieval World*, 1–14. Cardiff: University of Wales Press.

Smith, A. H. (ed.), 1935, *The Parker Chronicle (832–900)*. London: Methuen.

Smith, L. T. (ed.), 1907, *The Itinerary of John Leland: Parts I to III*. London: Bell.

——— (ed.), 1910, *The Itinerary of John Leland: Parts IX, X, and to XI*. London: Bell.

Smyth, A. P., 1995, *King Alfred the Great*. Oxford: Oxford University Press.

Stancliffe, Clare, 1995, 'Where Was Oswald Killed?', in Clare Stancliffe and Eric Cambridge (eds), *Oswald: Northumbrian King to European Saint*, 84–96. Stamford: Shaun Tyas.

———, 2010, 'British and Irish Contexts', in Scott DeGregorio (ed.), *The Cambridge Companion to Bede*. 69–83. Cambridge: Cambridge University Press.

Stenton, F. M., 1959, 'The East Anglian Kings of the Seventh Century', in Peter Clemoes (ed.), *The Anglo-Saxons*, 43–52. London: Bowes and Bowes.

———, 1971, *Anglo-Saxon England*, 3rd edn. Oxford: Clarendon.

Stevenson, W. H. (ed.), 1904, *Asser's Life of King Alfred*. Oxford: Clarendon.

Swanton, M. J. (tr.), 1996, *The Anglo-Saxon Chronicle*. London: Dent.

Thacker, Alan, 2010, 'Bede and History', in Scott DeGregorio (ed.), *The Cambridge Companion to Bede*, 170–89. Cambridge: Cambridge University Press.

Thomas, Charles, 1971, *Britain and Ireland in Early Christian Times*. London: Thames and Hudson.

———, 1981, *Christianity in Roman Britain*. Berkeley: University of California Press.

Thomas, R. J., 1933–35, 'Enwau Afonydd â'r ôlddodiad -*wy*', *Bulletin of the Board of Celtic Studies* 7, 117–33.

———, 1938, *Enwau Afonydd a Nentydd Cymru*. Caerdydd: Gwasg Prifysgol Cymru.

Toller, J. Northcote (ed.), 1898, *An Anglo-Saxon Dictionary*. Oxford: Clarendon.

Tolstoy, N., 1960–62, 'Nennius, Chapter Fifty-Six', *Bulletin of the Board of Celtic Studies* 19, 118–62.

Toop, Nicola, 2011, 'Northumbria in the West', in David Petts and Sam Turner (eds), *Early Medieval Northumbria*, 85–111. Turnhout: Brepols.

Wade-Evans, A. W. (ed.), 1944, *Vitae Sanctorum Britanniae*. Cardiff: University of Wales Press.

Vendryes, J., 1987, *Lexique étymologique de l'irlandais ancien: Lettre C*. Paris: Centre national de la recherche scientifique.

Venning, Timothy, 2013, *The Kings and Queens of Anglo-Saxon England*. Stroud: Amberley.

Wallace-Hadrill, J. M., 1988, *Bede's 'Ecclesiastical History of the English People': A Historical Commentary*. Oxford: Clarendon.

Wainwright, F. T., 1955, 'The Picts and the Problem', in F. T. Wainwright (ed.), *The Problem of the Picts*, 1–53. Edinburgh: Nelson.

Watson, W. J., 1926, *The History of the Celtic Place-Names of Scotland*. Edinburgh: Blackwood.

Watts, V. E., 2004, *The Cambridge Dictionary of English Place-Names*. Cambridge: Cambridge University Press.

Whitelock, Dorothy (ed.), 1967, *Sweet's Anglo-Saxon Reader*. Oxford: Clarendon.

——— (ed.), 1979, *English Historical Documents c. 500–1042*, 2nd edn. London: Eyre Methuen.

Williams, A. H., 1941, *An Introduction to the History of Wales: Prehistoric Times to 1063 AD*. Cardiff: University of Wales Press.

Williams, Hugh (ed.), 1899–1901, *Gildae de Excidio Britanniae*. London: Honourable Society of Cymmrodorion.

———, 1912, *Christianity in Early Britain*. Oxford: Clarendon.

Williams, Ifor, 1926–28, 'A Reference to the Nennian *Bellum Cocboy*', *Bulletin of the Board of Celtic Studies* 3, 59–62.

——— (ed.), 1935, *Canu Llywarch Hen*. Caerdydd: Gwasg Prifysgol Cymru.

——— (ed.), 1938, *Canu Aneirin*. Caerdydd: Gwasg Prifysgol Cymru.

———, 1939–41, 'Nodiadau ar Eiriau', *Bulletin of the Board of Celtic Studies* 10, 36–44.

———, 1944, *Lectures on Early Welsh Poetry*. Dublin: Dublin Institute for Advanced Studies.

———, 1945, *Enwau Lloeoedd*. Lerpwl: Gwasg y Brython.

——— (ed.), 1968, *The Poems of Taliesin*. Dublin: Dublin Institute for Advanced Studies.

———, 1972, *The Beginnings of Welsh Poetry*. Cardiff: University of Wales Press.

——— (ed.), 1972, *Armes Prydein*. Dublin: DIAS.

Williams, Mark, 2010, *Fiery Shapes*. Oxford: Oxford University Press.

Williams ab Ithel, J. (ed.), 1860, *Annales Cambriae*. London: Longman.

Wood, Ian, 1984, 'The End of Roman Britain', in Michael Lapidge and David Dumville (eds), *Gildas: New Approaches*, 1–25. Woodbridge: Boydell Press.

Wood, Michael, 2013, 'Searching for Brunanburh', *Yorkshire Archaeological Journal* 85, 138–59.

Woods, David, 2010, 'Gildas and the Mystery Cloud of 536–7'. *Journal of Theological Studies* 61, 226–34.

Woolf, Alex, 2004, 'Caedualla *Rex Brittonum* and the Passing of the Old North', *Northern History* 41, 5–24.

———, 2007, *From Pictland to Alba 789–1070*. Edinburgh: Edinburgh University Press.

Wormald, Patrick, 1982, 'The Ninth Century', in James Campbell (ed.), *The Anglo-Saxons*, 132–59. Oxford: Phaidon.

Yorke, Barbara, 2016, 'From Pagan to Christian in Anglo-Saxon England', in Roy Flechner and Máire Ní Mhaonaigh (eds), *The Introduction of Christianity into the Early Medieval Insular World*, 237–57. Turnhout: Brepols.

INDEX

Lightning Source UK Ltd.
Milton Keynes UK
UKHW021958250521
384363UK00006B/145